The Trails of M-22

40 of the Most Beautiful Paths Along Michigan's Most Beautiful Highway

By Jim DuFresne

MichiganTrailMaps.com

Published by
MichiganTrailMaps.com
P.O. Box 852
Clarkston, MI 48347
www.michigantrailmaps.com

Proudly Produced and Printed in Michigan of the United States of America

Editor: Phil Moldenhauer
Cover Design: Cislo Designs, Denver
Maps: MichiganTrailMaps.com
Printer: Color House Graphics, Grand Rapids

Cover photograph: *Hikers At Elberta Dunes South Natural Area* by Jim DuFresne
Title page photograph: *Arcadia Dunes Logs* by Angie Lucas
Page 2 photograph: *Arcadia Dunes Beach* by Nate Richardson
Page 13 photograph: *Fall Forest* by Nate Richardson
All other photos by the author unless otherwise credited.

www.michigantrailmaps.com

Scan the QR code for Michigan's best collection of trail maps designed for hiking, backpacking, mountain biking and Nordic skiing.

The Trails of M-22

Aspen leaves (photo by Angie Lucas).

Acknowledgements

My father was born on a cherry farm just outside of Elk Rapids. The DuFresnes have had a seasonal cottage in the village since 1922. During summers in high school, a friend and I lived in that century-old house and worked at a relative's cherry farm, shaking the tarts off the trees.

When Jennifer Jay of the Grand Traverse Regional Land Conservancy (GTRLC) approached me about writing a guidebook focusing on the trails along M-22, a road I've traveled and explored since I was old enough to walk, I couldn't imagine a more interesting way to spend a year. Or a better place to be based than the old family cottage in a corner of Michigan that I consider as much my home as anywhere else I've lived.

Simply put, the opportunity to research and write *The Trails of M-22* as part of the GTRLC 25th anniversary celebration was the kind of project that most writers only dream about. I am deeply appreciative to Jay and the entire GTRLC staff for their support, encouragement and contributions to the book. Likewise I am indebted to the staff of the Leelanau Conservancy, which also backed the project, especially Carolyn Faught.

I received considerable assistance, advice and time from Kerry Kelly of Friends of Sleeping Bear Dunes and Phil Akers, chief ranger at Sleeping Bear Dunes National Lakeshore. They were particularly helpful after the Great August Wind Storm in assessing what trails might be permanently closed and the extent of damage to others.

This area is so scenic that from the beginning we knew that *The Trails of M-22* had to be a full-color guidebook. Thus good photos were crucial and I'm honored that Ken Scott allowed us to grace many of the pages with his outstanding photography. Others contributing great images were Nate Richardson, Angie Lucas, Kathy Partin, Mary Centlivre, Carol Backman and Valerie van Heest, Michigan Shipwreck Association Director who provided the underwater photo of the City of Boston shipwreck.

Thanks to the gang at MichiganTrailMaps.com who kept this project moving along; Jessica, Michael, Jake, Melissa, Andree, Tom, Phil, Demetrios and Peg. Likewise I am indebted to Rick, Dave, Mark, Aurora and the entire staff of the Clarkston Post Office, where waiting in line is often the highpoint of my afternoon...and their's. This book could not have been possible without Steve, my yoga instructor from Yoga Oasis who never tires of reminding me to breathe, or Margaret, my yoga partner who is always there to tell me my cobra pose looks more like a garter snake lying in the sun.

Finally, this book is dedicated to the inspirational spirit of Andy. Get well my friend, for you and I belong out on the trail.

j.d.

The view of Lake Michigan from Baldy Trails in Arcadia Dunes (Grand Traverse Regional Land Conservancy photo).

Quintessential M-22

After a short hike from M-22, I was standing on the edge of Clay Cliffs, gazing at a postcard panorama of islands and perched dunes framed by the endless blue that is Lake Michigan, when suddenly soaring across the middle of it all was a bald eagle. At first I was mesmerized by the large raptor, then realized it wasn't the unexpected wildlife I was so enamored with.

It was M-22.

The 116-mile state highway that begins north of Manistee, ends in Traverse City and in between wraps around Michigan's little pinky like a glove, is constantly being crowned the nation's best autumn road trip or Michigan's most scenic drive. But more than simply a tourist slogan, M-22 is quintessential Northern Michigan, a spectacular landscape of dunes and orchards and beaches and vineyards surrounded by a freshwater sea and dotted with small towns and harbors. And while wine tasters, beach bunnies and leaf peepers follow the state highway in search of their sought-after indulgences, it is hikers, birders and other trail users who are truly blessed on a drive along this rolling ribbon of asphalt.

That's because the amount of public land surrounding M-22 is remarkable. The highway passes through the heart of Sleeping Bear Dunes National Lakeshore, the state's most popular national park with 71,000 acres of public land and 35 miles of beaches. It is also the gateway to more than two dozen preserves protected by the Grand Traverse Regional Land Conservancy (GTRLC) in Benzie County and the Leelanau Conservancy in Leelanau County. Add a nearby state park and rail-trails like the Leelanau Trail and it's easy to understand the reason for this guidebook.

There are no shortages of trails along this road.

M-22 is an original trunk line, a result of the 1913 Michigan Trunkline Highways Act. Spurred by the early car culture that emerged from Detroit, the act called for a 3,000-mile state highway system to be designated by townships and counties and built with financial help from the state. In 1919, the growing highway system was organized by numbers, with designers placing a block "M" at the top of a white diamond, adding the assigned highway number below it and encasing everything in black. Travelers have been following that iconic M-22 road sign ever since.

There have been modifications to the highway over the years. In 1920, M-22 began in Manistee and followed a route that is now US-31 before swinging toward the shoreline. M-109 through the heart of Sleeping Bear Dunes was originally M-22 before the highway was realigned to Glen Arbor in 1922 after the construction of a bridge across the Glen Lake narrows. In

The Trails of M-22

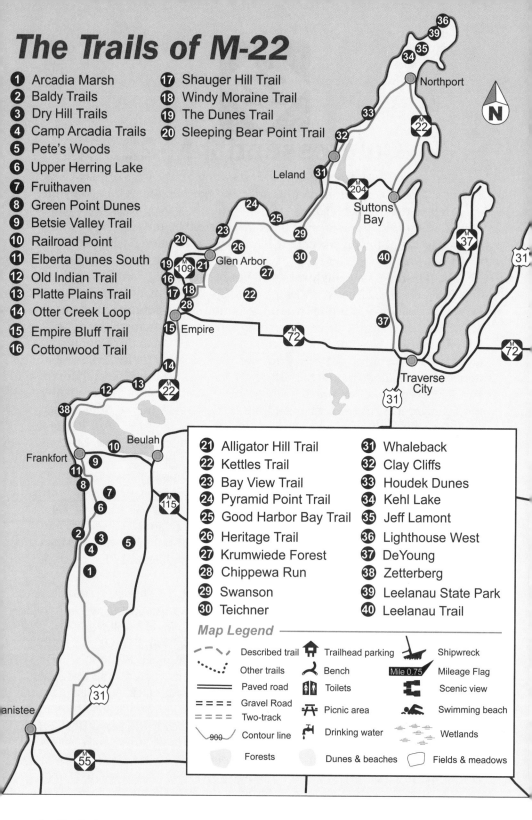

1. Arcadia Marsh
2. Baldy Trails
3. Dry Hill Trails
4. Camp Arcadia Trails
5. Pete's Woods
6. Upper Herring Lake
7. Fruithaven
8. Green Point Dunes
9. Betsie Valley Trail
10. Railroad Point
11. Elberta Dunes South
12. Old Indian Trail
13. Platte Plains Trail
14. Otter Creek Loop
15. Empire Bluff Trail
16. Cottonwood Trail
17. Shauger Hill Trail
18. Windy Moraine Trail
19. The Dunes Trail
20. Sleeping Bear Point Trail

21. Alligator Hill Trail
22. Kettles Trail
23. Bay View Trail
24. Pyramid Point Trail
25. Good Harbor Bay Trail
26. Heritage Trail
27. Krumwiede Forest
28. Chippewa Run
29. Swanson
30. Teichner
31. Whaleback
32. Clay Cliffs
33. Houdek Dunes
34. Kehl Lake
35. Jeff Lamont
36. Lighthouse West
37. DeYoung
38. Zetterberg
39. Leelanau State Park
40. Leelanau Trail

Map Legend

Symbol	Description	Symbol	Description	Symbol	Description
	Described trail		Trailhead parking		Shipwreck
	Other trails		Bench	Mile 0.75	Mileage Flag
	Paved road		Toilets		Scenic view
	Gravel Road		Picnic area		Swimming beach
	Two-track		Drinking water		Wetlands
	Contour line				
	Forests		Dunes & beaches		Fields & meadows

1936, M-22 to Suttons Bay was relocated along the west arm of the Leelanau Peninsula, next to Grand Traverse Bay, from its original route of Cherry Bend and Center roads. And in 1945, the last gravel stretch was paved.

What hasn't changed, however, is the landscape and that road sign pointing north.

Two things give the region encompassed by M-22 its distinct character: the 45th Parallel that cuts across it and the freshwater sea, the result of glaciers, that surrounds it. The 45th Parallel, marking halfway between the Equator and the North Pole, puts M-22 on the same latitude as some of the world's great wine country, including France's Bordeaux, and gives it that four-season climate that in October ignites the Northern mesic hardwood forests into flaming reds, golds and oranges. The area's trademark sand dunes, shoreline bluffs, ridges and inland lakes are often the result of the glaciers that scooped out Lake Michigan 11,000 years ago.

While all the natural beauty can be enjoyed on a road trip, to really appreciate this special slice of Michigan you need to stop at a trailhead, lace up the hiking boots and leave your vehicle, and your worries, behind. Only then can you pause on the edge of a towering bluff to watch a bald eagle soar over Lake Michigan and — far from the highway itself — experience quintessential M-22.

How To Use This Book

The 40 trails in this book have been organized into four sections. The first is devoted to the GTRLC preserves, the second to the trails in Sleeping Bear Dunes National Lakeshore, the third to Leelanau Conservancy preserves and the fourth section includes other trails.

Each trail begins with a quick-glance information box that includes distance, difficulty, hiking time and the GPS coordinates at the trailhead. At the top of every box is a series of quick-glance icons that provide additional information about amenities and trail usage. The icons are:

 Drinking water is available at the trailhead or on the trail

 Backcountry campground or a public campground is nearby

 Picnic area at the trailhead

 Trail features dunes

 The trail is open to mountain or road bikes.

 Swimming beach along the trail or near the trailhead

 Mountain biking is banned or strongly discouraged

 Birding opportunities

 Destination for Nordic skiers or snowshoers

 Trail features interpretive or historic displays

The 40 trail maps are based on GIS coordinates, USGS topographical data, satellite imagery and good old fashion field research. Larger, more detailed maps for every trail in this book are also available from the MichiganTrailMaps.com website (*www.michigantrailmaps.com*) and can be downloaded as a PDF file for use on a smartphone or tablet or printed.

Walking sticks left behind at the Whaleback Natural Area trailhead.

Those Who Preserve

The beauty of Northwest Michigan's M-22 corridor is far from a secret. This scenic 116-mile stretch of pavement that begins in Manistee County and ends in the corner of Leelanau County is at once a source of pride for locals and a favorite destination for scores of visitors every year.

And while M-22 has long been known for the splendid drive it offers, it's getting well-deserved attention for the many miles of public trails that allow us to best immerse ourselves in the sights, sounds and beauty of Northwest Michigan. These trails – established and maintained by organizations with a keen focus on preserving the region's unique natural character – truly shouldn't be overlooked.

Many of the trails featured in this guide exist on lands protected by The Grand Traverse Regional Land Conservancy and the Leelanau Conservancy, two non-profit entities dedicated to permanently protecting natural, scenic and farm lands. GTRLC, founded in 1991, works in Manistee and Benzie counties – home to the exquisite southern half of M-22 – along with Grand Traverse, Kalkaska and Antrim counties. The Leelanau Conservancy, established in 1988, covers all of Leelanau County and the northern half of M-22 as it snakes around the edge of the county and ends in the southwest corner of West Grand Traverse Bay.

Together, these conservancies have protected roughly 50,000 acres of land – that's about 78 square miles. They manage a combined 58 nature preserves and natural areas, and have protected and/or manage more than 100 miles of trail. Both organizations were born of a desire to protect northwest Michigan's natural treasures from continually increasing development pressure, and their work over more than two decades has provided northern Michigan residents and visitors with some of the most spectacular natural areas around.

GTRLC's centerpiece and largest property is Arcadia Dunes: The C.S. Mott Nature Preserve. This 3,600 acre preserve, with land in Benzie and Manistee counties, offers breathtaking views of Lake Michigan from a towering dune known as Old Badly and a series of excellent hiking and biking trails. At Green Point Dunes, a smaller parcel just north of Arcadia, visitors can hike through a rolling, mature hardwood forest on their way to a pair of fantastic overlooks and a secluded beach that offers a rare treat – the wreck of the City of Boston, a large cargo ship that lies in the snorkel-friendly depth of about 10 feet.

The Leelanau Conservancy has 11 natural areas along or just off of M-22.

Two of the most popular are Whaleback and Clay Cliffs Natural Area. Both feature protected shoreline and observation platforms, offering spectacular views of Lake Michigan. The Manitou Islands as well as other iconic landmarks define Leelanau's unique shoreline. From DeYoung Natural Area near Traverse City to Kehl Lake at the tip of the peninsula to Chippewa Run in Empire, Leelanau Conservancy natural areas offer unique opportunities to hikers, snowshoers, skiers and birders.

Additional trails with magnificent views exist in Sleeping Bear Dunes National Lakeshore, one of only three national parks in the state and one of the most famous natural areas in the Midwest. More than one million visitors typically flock to this 71,000 acre park every year. Established in 1970, the park includes miles of undeveloped shoreline on the mainland as well as North and South Manitou islands.

This diverse set of 40 trails along the M-22 corridor offers something for everyone – and during all seasons. The varied terrain and views offer exceptional hiking for people of all ages and skill levels. Mountain biking is offered on some trails, and, like hiking, can be enjoyed by experts or those just starting out in this increasingly popular sport. There's rarely a lack of fresh snow all winter long, creating fantastic conditions for snowshoeing and cross-country skiing.

The corridor is also excellent for naturalists, attracting visitors from around the state and country. Several ecosystems are in play here, including mixed woodlands, marsh/wetlands, grasslands and the ecologically sensitive dunes. These provide homes to an abundance of threatened or endangered species, including the grasshopper sparrow, Pitcher's thistle, Caspian tern, red-shouldered hawk and Blanding's turtle, among many others. Birders in particular are spoiled by the number of uncommon birds in the area.

This guide provides you a list of some of the best trails in this area, complete with everything you'll need to know to plan your trip. Additional information about these trails can be found at MichiganTrailMaps.com (*www.michigantrailmaps.com*) or on the websites of the organizations that continue to protect the region's natural splendor; Grand Traverse Regional Land Conservancy (*www.gtrlc.org*), Leelanau Conservancy (*www. leelanauconservancy.org*), Sleeping Bear Dunes National Lakeshore (*www.nps. gov/slbe*) and TART Trails (*www.traversetrails.org*).

Grand Traverse Regional Land Conservancy

Blue flag irises growing along the trail in Arcadia Marsh Nature Preserve.

Arcadia Marsh
Nature Preserve

Arcadia Marsh	
Distance: 1 mile	
Hiking Time: 30 minutes	
Difficulty: Easy	
Highlights: Birding, Wildflowers, Wetlands	
Map Source: Arcadia Marsh Nature Preserve from MichiganTrailMaps.com	
Trailhead: **GPS**	N44° 29' 20.79" W86° 13' 51.26"

Great Lakes coastal marshes are herbaceous wetland communities located along the shoreline of those lakes and their major connecting rivers. Such marshes are the second-most productive ecosystem in the world, providing a spawning ground for more than 50 species of fish, sanctuary for mammals, including otters and mink, and a critical habitat for the migration, feeding, and nesting of waterfowl and shorebirds.

Too bad we destroyed so many of them. Primarily because of their location along the shorelines, it's estimated that more than 80 percent of the original Great Lakes marshes have been destroyed. Along Lake Michigan in the Lower Peninsula, about 15 remain today, which is the reason Grand Traverse Regional Land Conservancy put such a high priority on restoring and preserving Arcadia Marsh.

Located in Manistee County, the 400-acre marsh borders Arcadia Lake and is fed by Bowens Creek. In the late 1800s, a railroad grade was constructed through the marsh. Then, in the 1950s, the water level was lowered to improve agricultural potential and twice Bowens Creek has been diverted, resulting in a stream that was very shallow and heavily sedimented. Finally, the marsh was permanently impacted when M-22 was constructed across Arcadia Lake as a quarter-mile causeway perforated only by a narrow bridge.

Restoration began in 2010 after GTRLC acquired 155 acres within the marsh. Teaming up with a handful of other conservation groups, work focused on restoring flows within the natural channel of Bowens Creek by plugging previous diversions. A prescribed burn was staged to counter the infestations of invasive species and 6 acres of shallow, open water was created within the marsh to benefit migrating birds and spawning northern pike.

Today, Arcadia Marsh Nature Preserve extends over 273 acres on the doorstep of the village of Arcadia. Although the trail system is limited, the preserve has become a popular destination for birders due to the easy viewing of waterfowl and marsh-dependent migrants. As an old two-track,

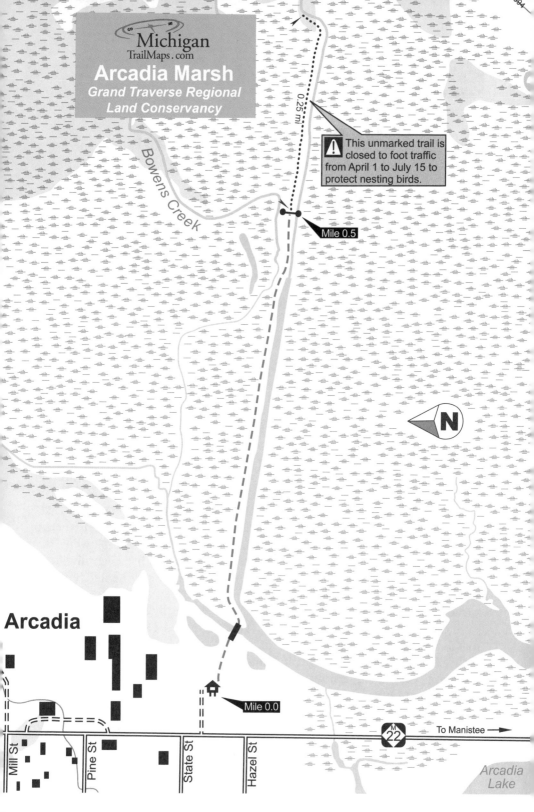

Michigan
TrailMaps.com
Arcadia Marsh
*Grand Traverse Regional
Land Conservancy*

0.25 mi

⚠ This unmarked trail is
closed to foot traffic
from April 1 to July 15 to
protect nesting birds.

Mile 0.5

Bowens Creek

N

Arcadia

Mile 0.0

Mill St

Pine St

State St

Hazel St

M-22   To Manistee →

Arcadia
Lake

the foot trail offers easy hiking, while M-22 can be used to scope nearly a mile of marsh by pulling off along the side of its elevated causeway.

Arcadia Marsh is home to more than 180 species of birds, including 17 State endangered, threatened, or species of special concern. In spring and fall, birders concentrate on migrating waterfowl, cranes (including sand hill cranes), and great blue and green herons. In low-water years the marsh is great for shorebirds and in high-water years it's one of the easiest places in Michigan to spot American and Least Bittern. Rarities that frequent the marsh include Marsh Wren, Northern Harrier, Common Moorhen, Trumpeter Swans, and Yellow-headed Blackbird, while in the winter birders often spot Rough-legged Hawks and migrating Short-eared Owls.

Access and Information

The preserve is located along M-22, a half mile south of the town of Arcadia with a trailhead and parking on the east side of the state highway. For more information, contact the Grand Traverse Regional Land Conservancy (231-929-7911; *www.gtrlc.org*).

On The Trail

The main trail at Arcadia Marsh is a wide mowed path that extends a half mile into the heart of the preserve. Other than an information kiosk, there are no other facilities at the trailhead. Dogs are not allowed from Feb. 1 to Sept. 1 and mountain bikes are banned from the trail.

The half-mile long maintained trail begins by crossing Bowen's Creek along a wide pedestrian bridge. Adjacent to the mowed path you will see an old water channel on the south and to the north is a vast sedge meadows which are prime nesting and foraging habitat for many listed bird species. Along the path, you may see native wildflowers that are beneficial pollinator plants, such as blue vervain, joe-pye weed, swamp milkweed and marsh skullcap.

Within a half mile you reach a gate across the two-track. Beyond it is a hard-to-follow trail through knee-high grass. This trail is closed from April 15 to July 15 — the reason for the gate — to protect the large number of birds nesting in the marsh. The trail continues east another quarter mile to where the channel empties into Bowens Creek.

Hikers beginning the climb to Old Baldy in Arcadia Dunes: The C.S. Mott Nature Preserve (photo by the Grand Traverse Regional Land Conservancy).

Baldy Trails

Arcadia Dunes: The C.S. Mott Nature Preserve

✺ ▲ ❄	
Baldy Trails	
Distance: 3.1 miles	
Hiking Time: 2 hours	
Difficulty: Easy	
Highlights: Old Baldy dune, Lake Michigan viewing points	
Map Source: Arcadia Dunes: Baldy Trails from MichiganTrailMaps.com or Grand Traverse Regional Land Conservancy at www.gtrlc.org	
Trailhead: **GPS** N44° 31' 33.38" W86° 13' 22.48"	

Even in a corner of Michigan where towering dunes are a common sight and miles of Lake Michigan shoreline are undeveloped, Arcadia Dunes is still an impressive preserve.

Officially known as the C.S. Mott Nature Preserve, Arcadia Dunes is spread across 3,800 acres straddling the Manistee/Benzie County line and is spilt in half by M-22. The preserve includes 2 miles of Lake Michigan shoreline, coastal bluffs with imposing perched dunes, hardwood forests, grasslands and more acreage than all but 13 state parks.

Other than a handful of gravel roads built in the late 1960s for a subdivision that never materialized, Acradia Dunes represented the largest remaining undeveloped tract of Lake Michigan coast when the Grand Traverse Regional Land Conservancy spearheaded a campaign to purchase the property. The fundraising effort culminated with the preserve being established in 2003. When the adjacent working farms, totaling an additional 2,000 acres, were also permanently protected, Arcadia Dunes became the largest conservation project ever completed by a local land trust in the Midwest.

Winding across much of the preserve are four trail systems — Dry Hill, Pete's Woods, Baldy and Camp Arcadia Trails — totaling almost 18 miles, with three of the four trailheads located just off M-22. Baldy Trails, the only system on the west side of the state highway, is a favorite among hikers. The 3.7-mile network of paths lead to Old Baldy, an open dune that rises 356 feet above Lake Michigan to provide sweeping views of the coastline.

You can reach the crown of Old Baldy in less than a mile but this 3.1-mile route along the perimeter of the system makes for an easy, two-hour to three-hour hike and includes all three viewing points. Mountain bikers are urged to bypass Baldy Trails — the open dunes and short segments make this system unsuitable for off-road cycling — and instead head across M-22 to the 10-mile Dry Hill Trails (see page 23).

Lake Michigan

Michigan
TrailMaps.com

Baldy Trails
Arcadia Dunes: The
C.S. Mott Nature Preserve

To Frankfort

M 22

875

825

908

957

Old Baldy
940 ft
Mile 1.8

Open Dunes
And Beach

Cable Steps

⚠ Warning: Steep
Bluffs prevent
access to the beach.

▲ 1040 ft

N

⑤

908

940

Mile 2.2

⑥ → ④
Mile 1.5

957

0.4 mi

0.4 mi

908

Mile 0.5 ③

Dry Hill
Trail

Mile 2.7 ⑦

⑧

②

M 22

Saint Pierre Rd

Camp
Trail

①
Mile 0.0
Mile 3.1

To
Arcadia

Matzinger Rd

924

Access and Information

Baldy Trailhead is posted along M-22, 8 miles south of Elberta or 2.7 miles north of Arcadia. If heading south, the trailhead entrance is on the west side of the state highway, 0.7 miles south of Joyfield Road. At the trailhead is an information kiosk and a porta john toilet but no source of drinking water.

For more information, contact the Grand Traverse Regional Land Conservancy (231-929-7911; *www.gtrlc.org*).

On The Trail

When followed in a counterclockwise direction, this loop begins as an easy and surprisingly level hike through a mature mesic hardwood forest carpeted in the spring with trillium and other wildflowers. Just down the trail is post No. 2 and by heading east (right) you reach post No. 3 at **Mile 0.5**, marking a junction with a short spur to a second trailhead on M-22.

At this point the loop heads northwest (left), climbs a bit, meanders and then at **Mile 1.5** descends to the first of two spurs that head north to the open dunes. Both merge at post No. 5 where a set of cable steps climb steeply out of the woods to the open dune that is Old Baldy.

Old Baldy is a perched dune, the result of wind blowing sand off the face of a bluff, not from the beach below, to the top of a glacial moraine. In Michigan, perched dunes are found along the northeastern shore of Lake Michigan and Lake Superior west of Grand Marais, featuring bluffs that often rise 90 feet to more than 400 feet above the water.

There is no beach access from the dune nor anywhere in the preserve because of the towering bluffs. But there are magnificent views. A sandy trail heads due north and at **Mile 1.8** reaches the 940-foot crown of Old Baldy. From this lofty "peak" you can spot the Frankfort Lighthouse along the Lake Michigan coastline and a portion of Lower Herring Lake, a panoramic view that rivals anything to the north in Sleeping Bear Dunes. Along the way a second trail heads west through a distinctive notch to an overlook of the lake and the perched dunes stretching to the south.

The return to the trailhead begins by backtracking and descending the cable steps to post No. 5 and then continuing due south to post No. 6, reached at **Mile 2.2**. The trail to the south is an overgrown two-track, part of the unrealized subdivision development. The trail to the west (right) is a foot path. Always follow a foot path if you have a choice. Within 300 yards you'll hear the Lake Michigan surf if the day is windy and see glimpses of the Great Lake through the trees. The trail swings south to follow the edge of the bluff and downhill to post No. 7, reached at **Mile 2.7**. The post marks a short spur to an opening on the bluff with more views of Lake Michigan.

Just beyond the post the trail swings east and makes a steady descent as an old two-track, bottoming out at post No. 8. Head right on the two-track at the junction and the entrance drive will be quickly reached and followed to the parking area.

A mountain biker on Dry Hill Trails (Grand Traverse Regional Land Conservancy photo).

3

Dry Hill Trails
Arcadia Dunes: The C.S. Mott Nature Preserve

⊛ Dry Hill Trails
Distance: 9.9 miles
Biking Time: 2-4 hours
Difficulty: Intermediate
Highlights: Single track, Rolling hardwood forests
Map Source: Arcadia Dunes: Dry Hill Trails from MichiganTrailMaps.com or Grand Traverse Regional Land Conservancy at www.gtrlc.org
Trailhead: **GPS** N44° 31' 32.02" W86° 12' 51.01"

The bulk of the Arcadia Dunes trail system is Dry Hill Trails, a glacial moraine that runs inland several miles from Lake Michigan. South of the moraine are forested back dunes and together they give the preserve a rugged interior, much to the delight of the mountain bikers who laid out the trail.

Although open to all trail users, Dry Hill was a collaboration between the Grand Traverse Regional Land Conservancy and the International Mountain Biking Association. The loop is classic single track, a flowing trail rated "intermediate difficulty" with quick rolling hills, long uphill sections and naturally banked turns.

The main trailhead is located on St. Pierre Road, just off M-22, and the loop is marked with map posts in a clockwise direction. Dry Hill loop is 9.9 miles while Chestnut Trail, a nested loop, reduces the ride to 2.1 miles.

Dry Hill, which lies between the Herring Lakes to the north and the Lake Arcadia watershed to the south, picked up its name when early farmers discovered it was too high above the water table to drill a well. Eventually, more advanced techniques allowed deeper wells to be drilled and the flatter areas on top were farmed.

The main loop winds through a half-dozen meadows and a hardwood forest of predominately sugar maple and American beech, making it a stunning ride in the fall. If riding in a clockwise direction, the first half from the St. Pierre Road trailhead is often tight and technical in the woods while the second half is more flowing, with a 1.6-mile long downhill stretch after the trail tops off above 1,000 feet.

Hikers also enjoy the trail. If the nearly 10-mile loop is too much, you can spot a car at a small parking area near where Dryhill crosses Taylor Road and a second vehicle where it crosses Matzinger Road, a mile before the St. Pierre trailhead. That would make for a 4-mile trek along what many consider the most beautiful section of the loop.

Mountain bikers looking for a flatter ride should consider 3.7-mile Camp Arcadia Trails, which also departs from the St. Pierre Trailhead (see page 27).

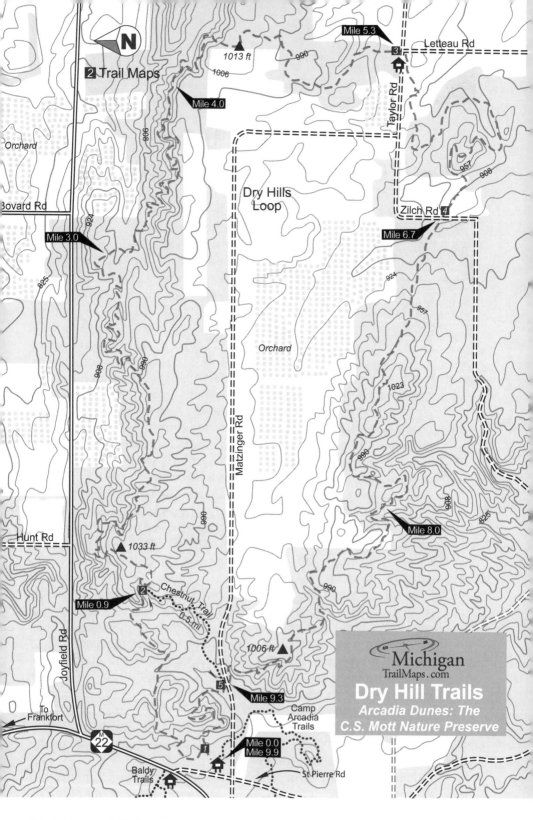

N

2 Trail Maps

1013 ft

1006

Mile 4.0

806

Bovard Rd

924

Mile 3.0

825

Orchard

Letteau Rd

Mile 5.3

3

Taylor Rd

957

908

Dry Hills Loop

Zilch Rd **4**

Mile 6.7

924

957

Orchard

1023

990

908

825

Mile 8.0

990

908

Matzinger Rd

996

Hunt Rd

1033 ft

2

Mile 0.9

Chestnut Trail 0.5 mi

990

1006 ft

990

5

Mile 9.3

Joyfield Rd

To Frankfort

22

Camp Arcadia Trails

1

Mile 0.0
Mile 9.9

St Pierre Rd

Baldy Trails

Michigan
TrailMaps.com
Dry Hill Trails
*Arcadia Dunes: The
C.S. Mott Nature Preserve*

Access and Information

The St. Pierre Trailhead for Dry Hill Trails is in the same vicinity as the Baldly Trailheads, 8 miles south of Elberta or 2.7 miles north of Arcadia. The trail is posted on the east side of M-22, a quarter mile south of Joyfield Road with trailhead parking located 100 yards south along the gravel St. Pierre Road. For more information, contact the Grand Traverse Regional Land Conservancy (231-929-7911; *www.gtrlc.org*).

On The Trail

From the parking area along St. Pierre Road, the trail quickly arrives at the first junction and posted map. Head north (left) to follow the loop in a clockwise direction. You enter the forest and within a half mile cross an old two-track and then climb one of the steeper hills of the day, arriving at map post No. 2 at *Mile 0.9*, the first junction with Chestnut Trail. Continue east (left) to continue with the Dry Hill loop.

The climbing continues for another quarter mile until you near 1,033 feet in elevation, Dry Hill's high point. After a rapid descent off the high point, the trail follows a pattern of quick dips in and out of the ravines along the northern edge of the moraine through *Mile 3*. Depending on the season, there might be quick views of orchards along the hillsides, vehicles rumbling by on Joyfield Road and even a glimpse of Upper Herring Lake.

Just beyond *Mile 4* the trail swings south and climbs sharply before topping off at 1,013 feet. A nearly mile-long long downhill run follows, descending more than 70 feet until you pop out at intersection of Taylor and Letteau Roads at *Mile 5.3*. Just to the west on the south side of Taylor Road is a small trailhead parking area.

After crossing Taylor Road the trail climbs a small knob and then curves back to descend its south side, bottoming out in a meadow and immediately climbing again. This time you reach an elevation of 973 feet and then embark on a fast, winding downhill run to map post No. 4 at Zilch Road, reached at *Mile 6.7*.

On the west side of Zilch Road the trail resumes climbing. This time it's a long steady ascent that at *Mile 7.5* tops off at 1,023 feet, the high point for the second half of the loop. Mountain bikers are well rewarded for the uphill effort as from there it's a fun downhill along a single track that follows the undulating crest of a ridge past small wooded hollows and ravines. Along the way you pass a physical milepost near *Mile 8*. This downhill run continues for 1.6 miles until you suddenly pop out at Matzinger Road. The dirt road appears so unexpectedly that caution is needed to avoid flying across it without first checking for oncoming traffic.

On the north side of at Matzinger Road is map post No. 5 and the second junction with the Chestnut Trail. Head left at the junction and the trail makes one more long climb before heading downhill for the St. Pierre Road trailhead, reaching it at *Mile 9.9*.

Brilliant fall colors along Camp Arcadia Trails (Photo by Nate Richardson).

Camp Arcadia Trails

Arcadia Dunes: The C.S. Mott Nature Preserve

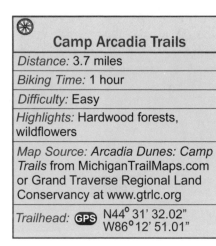

✲ Camp Arcadia Trails	
Distance: 3.7 miles	
Biking Time: 1 hour	
Difficulty: Easy	
Highlights: Hardwood forests, wildflowers	
Map Source: Arcadia Dunes: Camp Trails from MichiganTrailMaps.com or Grand Traverse Regional Land Conservancy at www.gtrlc.org	
Trailhead: **GPS**	N44° 31' 32.02" W86° 12' 51.01"

Complementing Dry Hill Trails in Arcadia Dunes: The C.S. Mott Nature Preserve and sharing the same trailhead is Camp Arcadia Trails.

Dry Hill, a nearly 10-mile loop, was designed by mountain bikers as an intermediate run of quick rolling hills and numerous long uphill sections. In contrast, Camp Arcadia Trails is a ride of only 3.7 miles and is laid out over fairly level terrain, making it much more appealing to those just getting into off-road cycling. Both are multi-use trails enjoyed by hikers much of the year and snowshoers in the winter.

Camp Arcadia Trails were built in 2014 with volunteer help from the trail's namesake Christian camp, Camp Arcadia. Located near the town of Arcadia, the camp was founded in 1922 when local lumber baron and dedicated Lutheran Henry Starke donated the land along Lake Michigan so families could enjoy "vacations with God."

Today, Camp Arcadia is owned by the Lutheran Camp Association and offers a wide range of activities from spring through fall, including mountain biking outings in Arcadia Dunes, just 3 miles away.

The 3.7-mile ride is an easy, non-technical outing through forests, open fields and old orchards but includes backtracking between the trailhead and a small loop. You can avoid doubling back through Abby's Woods and shortening the ride to 3 miles by following St. Pierre Road for a quarter mile back to the trailhead at the end.

Access and Information

Camp Arcadia Trails begins at the St. Pierre Trailhead, as does Dry Hill Trails, 8 miles south of Elberta or 2.7 miles north of Arcadia. The trail on the east side of M-22, a quarter mile south of Joyfield Road with trailhead parking located 100 yards south along St. Pierre Road, a gravel road.

For more information, contact the Grand Traverse Regional Land Conservancy at (231-929-7911; *www.gtrlc.org*).

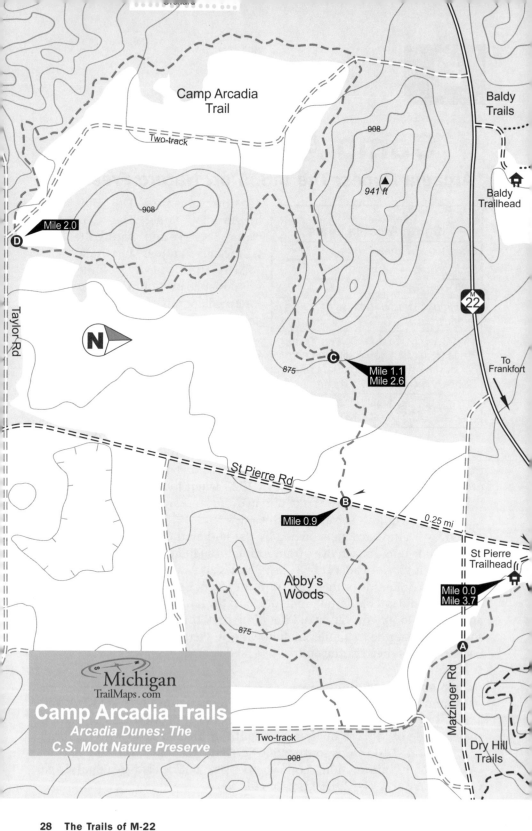

Camp Arcadia
Trail

Two-track

908

908

941 ft

Baldy
Trails

🏠

Baldy
Trailhead

Mile 2.0

D

Taylor Rd

N

M 22

To
Frankfort

875

C

Mile 1.1
Mile 2.6

St Pierre Rd

B

Mile 0.9

0.25 mi

St Pierre
Trailhead 🏠

Mile 0.0
Mile 3.7

Abby's
Woods

875

A

Matzinger Rd

Michigan
TrailMaps.com

Camp Arcadia Trails
*Arcadia Dunes: The
C.S. Mott Nature Preserve*

Two-track

908

Dry Hill
Trails

Spring trilliums in the woods along Camp Arcadia Trails.

On The Trail

At the trailhead there is parking, a porta john toilet in the summer and an information kiosk. Camp Arcadia Trails departs from the parking area as a winding single track, quickly crossing Matzinger Road before running parallel to an old farm lane, one of many crisscrossing the area. The trail is just inside a second-growth forest and skirts what used to be farm fields. At **Mile 0.3** you cross the two-track and the field to enter Abby's Woods.

Abby's Woods is a more mature forest with a slightly rolling terrain. In the spring the wildflowers are prolific. You break out of the trees to cross St. Pierre Road at post B, and cross another field to re-enter the woods, reaching Post C. This post, reached at **Mile 1.1**, marks the junction with the return trail. Take the fork to the right and within a third of a mile you'll be weaving through a forest on the edge of another former farm field, now an open meadow. The trail is just inside the trees as the meadow remains in view for more than a half mile.

At **Mile 2**, you cross another two-track and arrive at post D just to the north of Taylor Road. The trail skirts one more large meadow before entering the woods and arriving at post C at **Mile 2.6**. It's less than a quarter mile to St. Pierre Road, where you either backtrack through Abby's Woods for a 3.7-mile outing or follow the dirt road to reach the trailhead within minutes.

A fawn half hidden in Pete's Woods (Photo by Nate Richardson).

5

Pete's Woods
Arcadia Dunes: The C.S. Mott Nature Preserve

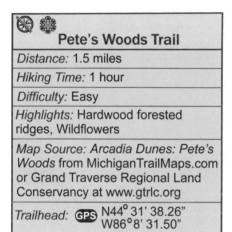

🧭 ❄️ Pete's Woods Trail	
Distance: 1.5 miles	
Hiking Time: 1 hour	
Difficulty: Easy	
Highlights: Hardwood forested ridges, Wildflowers	
Map Source: Arcadia Dunes: Pete's Woods from MichiganTrailMaps.com or Grand Traverse Regional Land Conservancy at www.gtrlc.org	
Trailhead: **GPS**	N44° 31' 38.26" W86°8' 31.50"

Anchoring the northeast corner of Arcadia Dunes: The C.S. Mott Nature Preserve, more than 4 miles from Lake Michigan, Pete's Woods lacks the impressive dunes or views of Baldy Trails or the miles of single track that mountain bikers crave at Dry Hill Trails. But come May, there is not a better place to experience the explosion of spring wildflowers than this patch of rugged woods.

The 135-acre tract may be reached via Swamp Road, but Pete's Woods is a second-growth, beech-maple forest crowned by century-old trees.

Stewardship of the preserve includes the removal of garlic mustard, an invasive species, which improves the diversity of the forest's understory. In short, more wildflowers. During the brief window between spring thaw and summer leaf-out – between late April and early June – blooms range from spring beauty and Dutchman's breeches to squirrel corn, yellow trout lily and bellwort. Trilliums are a given. So are morel mushrooms.

The preserve is named after Pedro Rodriguez, who with his wife, Iva, owned the forested ravines and adjoining farm where they grew corn for cattle from 1928 to 1971. Consumer's Power purchased the land in 1971 and the Grand Traverse Regional Land Conservancy permanently protected Pete's Woods in 2005 as part of Arcadia Dunes.

Pete's Woods Trail is a 1.5-mile loop up and around a forested ridge. The landscape is hilly but the hiking is surprisingly easy as the gradual climbs follow the natural contours of the ridge. Mountain bikes are banned at Pete's Woods and off-road cyclists are encouraged to ride at nearby Dry Hill Trails (see page 23) a trail system designed for them.

If Swamp Road is passable, Pete's Woods is a delightful snowshoe trek, and in October the northern hardwood forests make it a place to view fall colors. But the biggest attraction is in spring when the fantastic wildflower display is unparalleled.

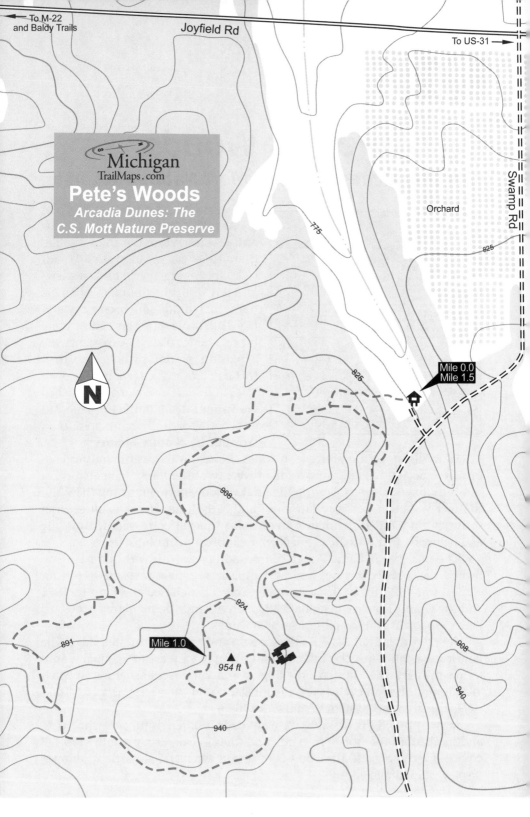

To M-22
and Baldy Trails

Joyfield Rd

To US-31 →

Michigan
TrailMaps.com

Pete's Woods
*Arcadia Dunes: The
C.S. Mott Nature Preserve*

Orchard

Swamp Rd

775

825

825

N

Mile 0.0
Mile 1.5

908

924

Mile 1.0

891

▲
954 ft

908

940

940

Dutchman's Breeches is one of many wildflowers hikers enjoy in Pete's Woods.

Access and Information

From Elberta, head south on M-22 for 7.3 miles and then east on Joyfield Road. Swamp Road is 3.5 miles to the east from M-22 or 1.7 miles west of US-31. The dirt road heads south past orchards before plunging into a wooded ravine as a rutted two-track and passing the Pete's Woods trailhead within a third of a mile from Joyfield Road. At the trailhead is an information kiosk but no toilets or source of drinking water.

For more information, contact the Grand Traverse Regional Land Conservancy (231-929-7911; *www.gtrlc.org*).

On The Trail

From the parking area, you cross the end of Pedro Rodriguez's old farm field and pass the red and white pines he planted in the 1950s. The trail then begins to climb the forested ridge and quickly reaches the junction with the return trail. Following the right-hand fork to the west, the trail continues to gradually ascend the ridge — if the wildflowers are out you'll hardly notice the climb.

Eventually, the trail swings due south and then east and at **Mile 0.8** you realize how rugged the preserve is. From the trail you can peer into a steep wooded hollow where more than 100 feet below is Swamp Road snaking through the woods.

At this point the trail swings around the high point of the ridge at 954 feet and at **Mile 1** begins its steady descent back to the trailhead. Within a third of a mile the trail bottoms out just above Swamp Road and parallels the two-track back to the junction that was passed at the beginning of the hike.

Blue herons are among the many species of birds seen at Upper Herring Lake.

6

Upper Herring Lake
Nature Preserve

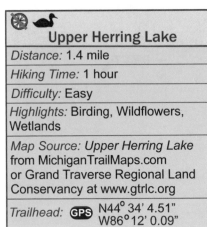

Upper Herring Lake	
Distance: 1.4 mile	
Hiking Time: 1 hour	
Difficulty: Easy	
Highlights: Birding, Wildflowers, Wetlands	
Map Source: Upper Herring Lake from MichiganTrailMaps.com or Grand Traverse Regional Land Conservancy at www.gtrlc.org	
Trailhead: GPS N44° 34' 4.51" W86° 12' 0.09"	

Birds like a variety of habitats. Birders like to see a variety of birds. Everybody – birds and those who watch them – seems to like Upper Herring Lake Nature Preserve.

Transferred in 1991 to the Grand Traverse Regional Land Conservancy, the 180-acre tract is highlighted by a nearly mile-long trail that winds through five habitats: old field, planted pine, young northern forest, northern wet meadow and northern shrub swamp, before ending in a small upland section surrounded by marl pit ponds.

It's this variety of habitats that allows Upper Herring Lake to provide a variety of birding opportunities. In the spring visitors can listen for bitterns and rails in the wet meadow and shrub swamp or spot woodcock darting overhead in the old fields. Waterfowl gather in the marl pit ponds while sandhill cranes are among the birds that nest there.

The heart of the preserve is the 2,800 feet of frontage along the west side of Upper Herring Lake. The 542-acre lake is connected to Lower Herring Lake via Herring Creek with M-22 extending north between them.

Access and Information

The trailhead for Upper Herring Lake Nature Preserve is posted along M-22, 4.3 miles south of Elberta or 3.6 miles north of the Arcadia Dunes-Baldy Trailhead. The preserve sign and parking lot is on the east side of the road, next to an old schoolhouse. There are no facilities at the trailhead other than parking.

For more information, contact the Grand Traverse Regional Land Conservancy (231-929-7911; *www.gtrlc.org*).

On The Trail

Most of the Upper Herring Lake Trail is a two-track that heads east from the trailhead parking area into a lightly forested area and then swings south

To US-31

604

Herron Rd

Herring Creek

Upper Herring Lake

Mile 0.7

Marl Pit Ponds

Boardwalk

600

Mile 0.4

610

610

Michigan
TrailMaps.com

Upper Herring Lake
*Grand Traverse Regional
Land Conservancy*

610

N

Herring Lake
Church

To
Frankfort

Mile 0.0
Mile 1.4

M-22

To Arcadia →

Paddling Upper Herring Lake

A popular way to explore Upper Herring Lake Nature Preserve is by paddling canoes and kayaks. A DNR boat ramp is located on Herron Road at the north end of the 542-acre lake, just east of its outlet with Herring Creek. The creek meanders northwest and then southwest before ending its 2.5-mile journey by emptying into the northeast corner of Lower Herring Lake. Together, the lakes offer 1,022 acres of surface area.

Upper Herring Lake has more than 5 miles of shoreline, with most paddlers heading south to explore the west side of the lake. Part of the Grand Traverse Regional Land Conservancy preserve, this stretch of shoreline is an extensive wetland area and lends itself well to spotting kingfishers, herons and a variety of waterfowl.

Paddlers can enjoy additional birding opportunities by following Herring Creek. The creek is navigable for 1.6 miles from the DNR launch to the M-22 bridge, a leisurely hour-long paddle. Beyond the bridge, Herring Creek is usually too shallow and clogged with fallen trees to explore. To paddle Lower Herring Lake, put in at a DNR boat launch reached from M-22 by heading west on Elberta Resort Road.

through meadows and a fallow field. In less than a half mile the two-track ends and gives way to a true foot path that enters a birch forest and quickly arrives at the preserve's boardwalk.

The 900-foot boardwalk is an impressive structure as it winds through a northern shrub swamp and wet meadow, providing views in every direction while keeping your boots dry. At *Mile 0.7*, the boardwalk reaches a forested upland area, with a foot path leading to the edge of the historic marl pit ponds.

Marl is a lime-rich mud, a mixture of clay and carbonate of lime. In the late 1800s and early 1900s, farmers excavated marl from pits like these and used it as fertilizer in their sandy fields. The marl may have been free but marling was labor-intensive and once alternative fertilizers became readily available the practice soon disappeared.

From the marl pit ponds, the only way back to the trailhead is to backtrack.

A dark eyed junco is framed by fall colors (photo by Angie Lucas).

Fruithaven
Nature Preserve

Fruithaven
Distance: 0.7 mile
Hiking Time: 30 minutes
Difficulty: Easy
Highlights: Hardwood forested ridge, Fall colors
Map Source: Fruithaven Nature Preserve downloaded from MichiganTrailMaps.com or Grand Traverse Regional Land Conservancy at www.gtrlc.org
Trailhead: ⊕ GPS N44° 34' 25.31" W86° 11' 21.06"

For more than 50 years since William McKinley purchased 551 acres north of Upper Herring Lake in 1945, his family operated Fruithaven Orchard on a spread that was a mix of orchards, fields and forested ridges.

When the McKinleys were ready to give up their agrarian way of life in the late 1990s, developers from southern Michigan made an offer to purchase the farm with plans to build a pair of 18-hole golf courses, hotel and an airstrip.

Sparing the area from commercial development was paramount to the Grand Traverse Regional Land Conservancy (GTRLC). The conservancy first convinced the family to apply for Purchase of Development Rights funds through the state of Michigan. But when the application process dragged on, GTRLC stepped in and purchased the property. Eventually, the development rights to 360 acres of farmland were sold to ensure the land stays in agricultural production. But 176 acres was designated as Fruithaven Forest Reserve, now known as Fruithaven Nature Preserve.

Fruithaven is linked with GTRLC's Upper Herring Lake Nature Preserve — together they protect 256 acres of the Herring Lakes Watershed. Other than an old farm field and the hardwood wetlands in the Herring Creek floodplain, Fruithaven is a broken terrain of ridges and valleys covered by a mesic northern forest of predominately sugar maples, American beech and hemlocks. Wildlife that might be encountered ranges from whitetail deer and coyotes to wild turkeys, indigo buntings and pileated woodpeckers.

Originally, Fruithaven was accessed by nearly 2 miles of existing two-tracks. But the old forest roads were poorly marked, hard to follow and required backtracking. In 2014, a 0.7-mile loop was built from the trailhead on Herron Road that utilizes only a short segment of a two-track. While the loop features almost 100 feet in elevation, the climbs are gentle and reward hikers, and snowshoers, with a glimpse of the wetlands that Herring Creek flows through.

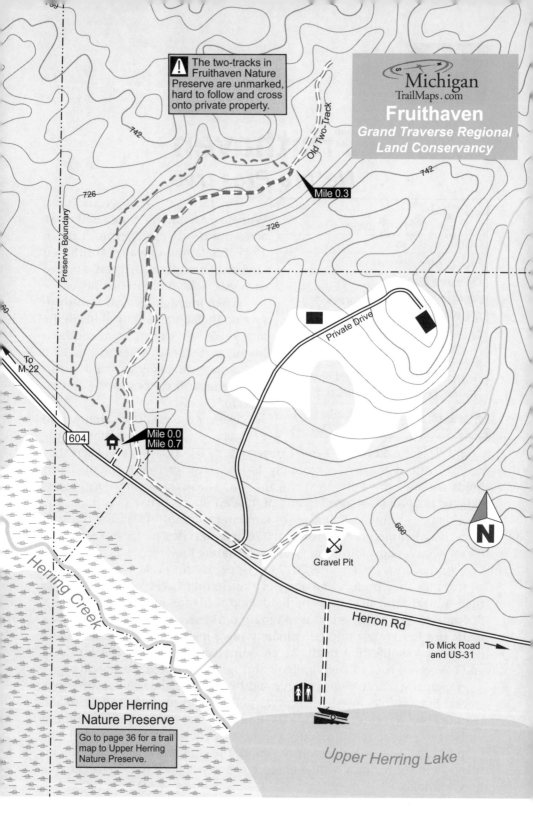

⚠ The two-tracks in Fruithaven Nature Preserve are unmarked, hard to follow and cross onto private property.

Michigan
TrailMaps.com
Fruithaven
Grand Traverse Regional Land Conservancy

Old Two-Track

Mile 0.3

742

726

726

742

Preserve Boundary

Private Drive

660

To M-22

604

Mile 0.0
Mile 0.7

N

Gravel Pit

Herron Rd

To Mick Road and US-31

Herring Creek

Upper Herring Nature Preserve

Go to page 36 for a trail map to Upper Herring Nature Preserve.

Upper Herring Lake

The hardwood forested ridges of Fruithaven Nature Preserve make it a wonderful destination for a fall hike (photo by Angie Lucas).

Access and Information

From M-22, turn east on Herron Road (also labeled County Road 604) and within a mile the posted trailhead for Fruithaven Nature Preserve is on the north side of the road. From US-31, turn west on Mick Road, also labeled CR-604. Follow CR-604 for 5 miles to the trailhead. In the winter there can be significant snow accumulation in the parking area, so snowshoers occasionally park on the south side of Herron Road.

For more information, contact the Grand Traverse Regional Land Conservancy at (231-929-7911; *www.gtrlc.org*).

On The Trail

There is an information sign and parking near the trailhead but no other facilities. A well-marked path heads north into a narrow valley and within a couple hundred yards merges into a forested two-track from the east. The trail is level at the beginning but enclosed on both sides by nearly 100-foot high ridges, a sign of things to come.

At *Mile 0.3*, the trail veers off the two-track and immediately climbs the ridge to the west. The climb is gentle and gradual. You never reach the crest of the ridge but rather sidle the steep east side of it before the trail begins a steady descent to the trailhead. Along the way you pass a glimpse of the extensive Herring Creek wetlands if the foliage is not too thick and then pop out at the parking area at *Mile 0.7*.

Enjoying the view of Lake Michigan from a viewing deck at Green Point Dunes.

8

Green Point Dunes
Nature Preserve

🎡 🚶 ⛰ 🏊	
Green Point Dunes	
Distance: 2 miles	
Hiking Time: 1 to 2 hours	
Difficulty: Easy	
Highlights: Beach, shipwreck, Lake Michigan vistas	
Map Source: Green Point Dunes Nature Preserve downloaded from MichiganTrailMaps.com or Grand Traverse Regional Land Conservancy at www.gtrlc.org	
Trailhead: **GPS**	N44° 35' 24.03" W86° 12' 54.35"

A half mile into the hike at Green Point Dunes Nature Preserve is the first observation deck overlooking Lake Michigan. Just beyond that is the second deck, offering one of the most dramatic views along M-22.

From that perch, hikers can gaze at a long, sweeping beach to the south leading to open dunes towering above the shoreline. Straight below in the clear waters of Lake Michigan are the remains of a steamer that ran aground in 1873. And if you arrive late in the day, you can sit on the bench and watch the sun fade into a watery horizon.

Sand dunes, shipwrecks and sunsets – Green Point Nature Preserve is one of Grand Traverse Regional Land Conservancy's most impressive efforts.

Acquired in 2005, the 242-acre preserve south of Elberta in Benzie County contains nearly 3 miles of trails that wind through open meadows and stands of a brilliant white birch, beech-maple forest that is carpeted with wildflowers in the spring. But it is the 2,100-plus feet of Lake Michigan shoreline and the high bluff bordering much of it that makes Green Point Dunes so spectacular.

The vistas are the result of a glacial moraine extending east to west and separating the Herring Lakes watershed to the south from the Betsie River watershed to the north. From Lake Michigan, the steep ridge rises 274 feet, more than enough elevation for dramatic views of distant shorelines in each direction.

Almost half of the preserve has been labeled by the state as "critical dune," a designation to protect fragile dune areas. At Green Point, the dune habitat includes forested dunes, open foredunes that are home to the state- and federally-threatened Pitcher's Thistle and wide sandy beaches.

The trail system at Green Point Dunes, the route described here, forms a 2-mile loop to the beach and includes all three viewing decks. Departing from a second trailhead along Green Point Road is a two-track that crosses

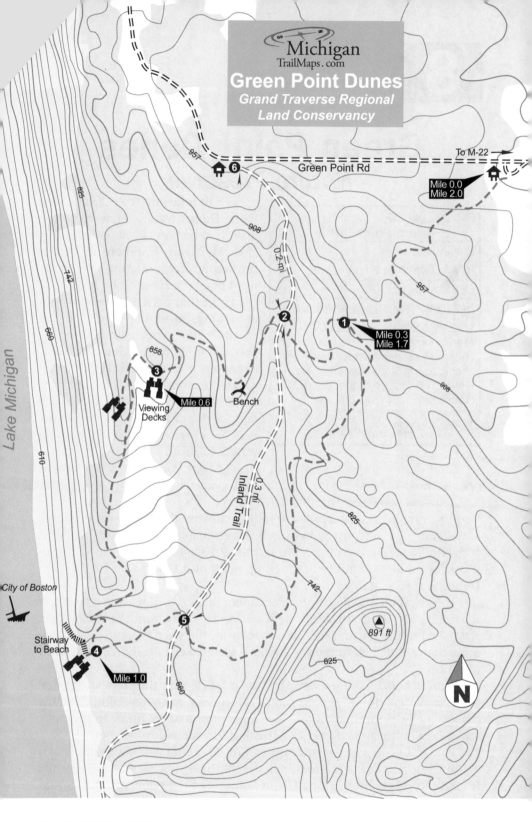

Michigan
TrailMaps.com
Green Point Dunes
Grand Traverse Regional
Land Conservancy

Green Point Rd

To M-22

Mile 0.0
Mile 2.0

957

908

0.2 mi

2

1

Mile 0.3
Mile 1.7

957

908

858

3

Mile 0.6

Bench

Viewing
Decks

825

742

660

610

Lake Michigan

0.3 mi

Inland Trail

825

742

891 ft

City of Boston

Stairway
to Beach

4

Mile 1.0

5

660

825

N

the preserve to private property south of it. The two-track, occasionally referred to as the Inland Trail, is closed to vehicles but hikers can use it to reduce this trek to 1.5 miles while still reaching the observation decks and beach.

Access and Information

From Frankfort, head south on M-22 and in 4.3 miles turn west (right) on Green Point Road. In less than a quarter mile the main trailhead will be on the south side of the road. In another quarter mile is the trailhead for the two-track.

For more information, contact the Grand Traverse Regional Land Conservancy (231-929-7911; *www.gtrlc.org*).

On The Trail

At the main trailhead, there is parking for a dozen cars and an information kiosk but no source of drinking water.

The trail crosses a small meadow and then begins a steady climb of a forested ridge. Topping off in a quarter mile, you can see a sliver of Lake Michigan blue through the trees in early spring or late fall, teasing you of what lies ahead. The trail descends through the rolling terrain and at **Mile 0.3** reaches post No. 1 at the junction of the return trail. The descent continues to post No. 2, marking the junction with the two-track, or Inland Trail, before the climbing resumes.

You pass an inviting log bench on the way up and then at **Mile 0.6** reach post No. 3 and the first deck. The view includes the large open meadow that occupies the middle of the preserve, the Lake Michigan shoreline and to the south, Lower Herring Lake. After another dip and climb you arrive at the short spur that leads to the second deck, where an hour or even two can easily be spent. The vistas are that impressive.

To the south is a much better view of the shoreline, Lower Herring Lake and Baldy, the towering open dunes that are part of Arcadia Dunes/C.S. Mott Nature Preserve (see page 19). To the north, the shoreline leads to the Frankfort Lighthouse. And below is the City of Boston, the ship that ran aground in 1873. The outline of the steamer's bow is just to the south of the observation platform and clearly visible when Lake Michigan is calm and the shifting sands cooperate.

The main trail continues south along the edge of the glacial ridge before descending rapidly to post No. 4, reached at **Mile 1**, marking another platform and the massive stairway to the beach. Depending on the water level, the beach is wide and beautiful. Those who pack a bathing suit, mask and snorkel can spend an afternoon exploring the shipwreck.

The two-track is reached within a few hundred yards from the stairway at post No. 5 and is followed by a steady uphill march to the top of the glacial moraine, a climb of 232 feet. You top off near post No. 1 at **Mile 1.7** and from there backtrack the first leg of the hike to the trailhead.

The Sinking of the *City of Boston*

The bow of the City of Boston shipwreck, photo by Valerie van Heest, MSRA Director

Built in Cleveland in 1863 for the Northern Transportation Co. of Ohio, the *City of Boston* was a 136-foot-long wooden steamer with an engine and propeller but also a mast and a history of bad luck.

Within four years of its christening, the ship ran aground in Chicago and three months later its engine failed and the vessel had to be towed to Milwaukee.

In 1868, the *City of Boston* collided with another steamer, the *Milwaukee*, and sank in the Straits of Mackinac. When the steamship was raised 125 feet two years later, it was the deepest salvage ever attempted in the Great Lakes at the time. After being towed and rebuilt in Cleveland, the ship returned to service as a steam barge only to finally meet its end in November, 1873 during a blinding snowstorm. The *City of Boston* was hauling flour and corn when it ran aground on a sand bar just off Green Point Dunes. The raging surf quickly broke the hull and the ship was abandoned by its crew while its cargo was a total loss.

Its boiler and engine were recovered in 1887 but the rest of the vessel is now one of the most popular shipwrecks along Lake Michigan. What remains of the steamship is located due west from the beach access stairway, 150 to 200 feet from shore depending on the water level. It's angled in 7 to 8 feet of water with its stern buried in the sand bar and its bow occasionally less than 4 feet below the surface of the lake.

The *City of Boston* is not alone — there are 20 other wrecks in the vicinity of Green Point Dunes Nature Preserve. For more information about the *City of Boston* or other wrecks along the Lake Michigan shoreline go to the Michigan Shipwreck Research Association (MSRA) web site at *michiganshipwrecks.org*.

The Betsie Lake boardwalk along the Betsie Valley Trail.

9&10

Railroad Point
and the Betsie Valley Trail

As the 20th century began, the Toledo, Ann Arbor and North Michigan Railway extended from the Ohio city to Elberta, where rail ferries transported the trains across Lake Michigan to Manitowoc, Wis., or Menominee in the Upper Peninsula.

When the trains departed nearby Beulah for Elberta, they followed Crystal Lake and within a few miles made a sharp swing southwest at a bend in the shoreline that locals referred to as Railroad Point. The name stuck even after rail service had disappeared by the 1980s. What eventually replaced the boxcars were cyclists, hikers and other trail users on one of the most scenic sections of the Betsie Valley Trail in an area that was eventually preserved as Railroad Point Natural Area.

Not only are the histories of the 22-mile rail-trail and the 200-acre natural area interwoven but so is the popularity of their trails. Six miles of the rail-trail, from Frankfort to the Mollineaux Road trailhead, are paved and less than a third of a mile away is the trailhead for Railroad Point. Today a favorite activity for many is a 14-mile bike-and-hike outing to the views of Crystal Lake from the bluffs in Railroad Point Natural Area.

A similar outing can also begin in Beulah, where a replica of the town's former railroad depot serves as a a trailhead for the Betsie Valley Trail. From

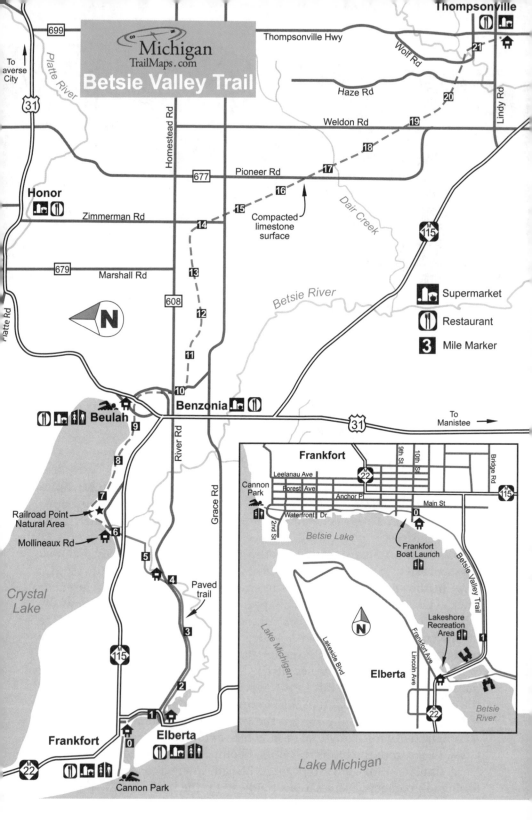

Michigan
TrailMaps.com
Betsie Valley Trail

To
averse
City

To
Traverse
City

699

Platte River

31

Thompsonville

Thompsonville Hwy

Wolf Rd

21

Haze Rd

20

Lindy Rd

Weldon Rd

19

Homestead Rd

Pioneer Rd

18

677

17

16

Compacted
limestone
surface

Dair Creek

Honor

Zimmerman Rd

15

14

115

679

Marshall Rd

13

608

12

Betsie River

Platte Rd

11

Supermarket

Restaurant

3 Mile Marker

10

Benzonia

31

To
Manistee

Beulah

9

8

7

Railroad Point
Natural Area

6

Mollineaux Rd

5

Crystal
Lake

River Rd

Grace Rd

4

Paved
trail

3

115

2

1

0

Frankfort

Elberta

Cannon Park

22

Frankfort

Leelanau Ave

Forest Ave

Anchor Pl

9th St

10th St

Bridge Rd

22

Cannon
Park

Main St

2nd St

Waterfront Dr

0

Frankfort
Boat Launch

115

Betsie Lake

Betsie Valley Trail

Lake Michigan

Lakeside Blvd

N

Lakeshore
Recreation
Area

Frankfort Ave

Lincoln Ave

1

Elberta

22

Betsie
River

Lake Michigan

there, it is a 4-mile ride to Mollineaux Road along a limestone aggregate trail that wraps around the shoreline of the point and is best suited for hybrids and mountain bikes. A hike to the views in the Railroad Point Natural Area and a return to Beulah is a 10-mile bike-and-hike outing.

Betsie Valley Trail

Built after the Michigan DNR purchased the abandoned rail corridor in 1998, the Betsie Valley Trail extends 22 miles from Frankfort to Thompsonville, passing through Beulah and Elberta and near Benzonia. Highlights for many are the 3-mile stretch along Crystal Lake and the numerous views of Betsie Lake and Betsie River.

Mile 0 of the trail is at 10th Street in Frankfort, where it officially becomes the DNR-owned Betsie Valley Trail. A connector trail continues west through Frankfort's waterfront parks on Betsie Lake and along Waterfront Drive for three blocks to provide access to the Lake Michigan beach in Cannon Park.

Betsie Valley Trail	
Distance: 22 miles	
Biking Time: 4-5 hours	
Difficulty: Moderate	
Highlights: Partially paved rail-trail, Crystal Lake, Betsie River	
Map Source: Betsie Valley Trail from MichiganTrailMaps.com or Friends of Betsie Valley Trail at www.betsievalleytrail.org	
Trailhead: GPS	N44° 37" 55.01" W86° 13' 41.96"

Access and Information

There are six designated trailhead parking areas for the Betsie Valley Trail, including on 10th Street just south of Main Street in Frankfort. Other trailheads, where parking is available, are at Mile 1 along M-22 in Elberta, at a DNR boat launch along River Road just past Mile 4, on the north side of Mollineaux Road at Mile 6, at the Beulah Visitors Center on Benzie Boulevard and at the trail's southern end in Thompsonville where there is parking at the ball field just north of Lindy Road (County Road 602).

Additional information on the trail is available from the web site of the Friends of the Betsie Valley Trail (*www.betsievalleytrail.org*) or the Benzie County Visitors Bureau (800-882-5801; *www.visitbenzie.com*).

On The Trail

The trail from Cannon Park to Mollineaux Road (6.7 miles) features an asphalt surface suitable for road bikes, inline skating and parents jogging with a young one in a carriage. The 10th Street trailhead is adjacent to the large Frankfort boat launch with restrooms and drinking water.

From 10th Street, the rail-trail skirts the south end of Betsie Lake past the **Mile 1** marker and then parallels M-22 briefly as it crosses Betsie River via a boardwalk with an observation area in the middle. At the west end of the boardwalk the trail arrives at the entrance of Lakeshore Recreation Area where there are toilets and picnic tables. A well marked crossing here leads you across M-22 to the Elberta trailhead on the other side. You then swing east to re-cross the mouth of the Betsie River a second time, passing another observation area.

For the next 3 miles the rail-trail parallels River Road and then crosses it at **Mile 4** to a DNR boat launch that serves as a trailhead. Additional views of the Betsie River are enjoyed before the trail crosses M-115 and arrives at the trailhead on Mollineaux Road. A third of a mile to the east on Mollineaux Road is the trailhead for the Mary Margaret Johnson Trail, the start of a short hike to views of Crystal Lake from Railroad Point Natural Area.

Beyond Mollineaux Road, Betsie Valley Trail switches to a limestone aggregate surface and for the next mile hugs the shoreline of Crystal Lake as it passes through the natural area. From the rail-trail there is easy access to the lake and a swimming area along this stretch. For the remaining 2 miles to Beulah the rail-trail winds through private property on a 10-foot easement where special-use restrictions, including a ban on dogs and a 10 mph speed limit, are posted. Within view of Crystal Lake most of the way, this portion of the Betsie Valley Trail can be very sandy in places.

At **Mile 9**, the Betsie Valley Trail enters Beulah and arrives at a replica of the town's former railroad depot that serves as a trailhead and visitor's center with information, maps, restrooms and drinking water. Restaurants and a public swimming beach are nearby.

Two blocks from the depot the Betsie Valley Trail crosses US-31. The aggregate trail swings south and then resumes its easterly direction at **Mile 10** with a gradual ascent for the next 5 miles to Aylsworth Road, much of it in the Pere Marquette State Forest. The trail crosses Dair Creek at **Mile 17**, where a wooden stairway descends to a beaver dam across the stream. Just before entering Thompsonville is an old turbine at Wolf Road that produced the first electricity in the area. The Betsie River is then crossed via a renovated railroad bridge and the rail-trail arrives at its east end on Thompson Avenue, one block south of Lindy Road.

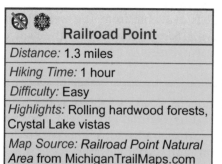

Railroad Point	
Distance: 1.3 miles	
Hiking Time: 1 hour	
Difficulty: Easy	
Highlights: Rolling hardwood forests, Crystal Lake vistas	
Map Source: Railroad Point Natural Area from MichiganTrailMaps.com or Grand Traverse Regional Land Conservancy at www.gtrlc.org	
Trailhead: **GPS** N44° 38' 15.66" W86° 8' 21.40"	

Railroad Point Natural Area

In 1998, with the help of the Grand Traverse Regional Land Conservancy, Benzie County secured a Michigan Natural Resources Trust Fund grant and purchased 66 acres on Railroad Point, the largest undeveloped parcel remaining on Crystal Lake. The natural area has been expanded twice, most recently in 2012, and now includes 209 acres that extends from the shores

The trail at Railroad Point in the fall (photo by Nate Richardson).

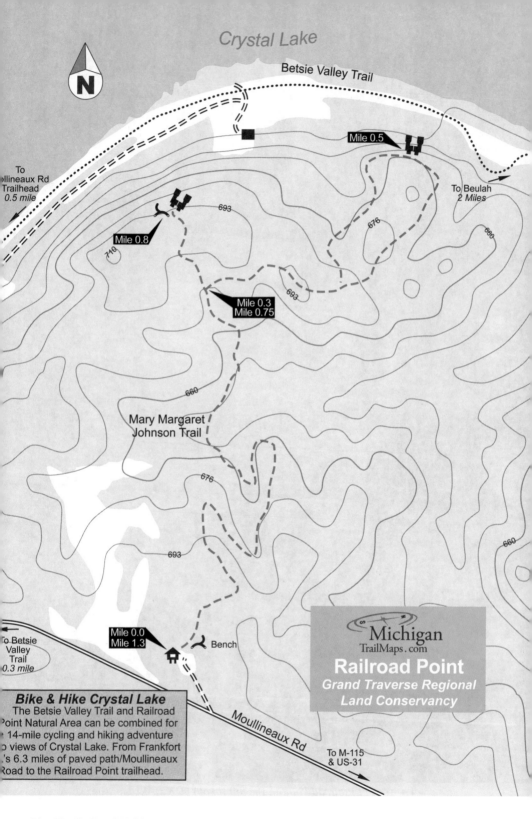

Crystal Lake

Betsie Valley Trail

N

Mile 0.5

To
ollineaux Rd
Trailhead
0.5 mile

To Beulah
2 Miles

693

676

660

Mile 0.8

710

693

Mile 0.3
Mile 0.75

660

Mary Margaret
Johnson Trail

676

693

660

Michigan
TrailMaps.com
Railroad Point
*Grand Traverse Regional
Land Conservancy*

To Betsie
Valley
Trail
0.3 mile

Mile 0.0
Mile 1.3

Bench

Moullineaux Rd

To M-115
& US-31

Bike & Hike Crystal Lake
The Betsie Valley Trail and Railroad
Point Natural Area can be combined for
14-mile cycling and hiking adventure
views of Crystal Lake. From Frankfort
's 6.3 miles of paved path/Moullineaux
Road to the Railroad Point trailhead.

of Michigan's ninth largest lake south to the Betsie River, a Natural and Wild-Scenic River.

When combined with the adjoining, state-owned Crystal property, the preserves protect 4,300 feet of lake frontage or m of Crystal Lake's publicly-owned shoreline. Inland Railroad P upland forests, wetlands, steep-sided bluffs and portions of Outle Creek, the warm-water stream that connects the lake to the Betsie River.

Such a diverse habitat supports an equally wide range of wildlife, from whitetail deer, bobcats, black bears, otters and coyotes to birds such as wild turkeys, great blue herons, wood ducks and the red-shouldered hawk, a threatened species in Michigan.

Two trails provide access into Railroad Point. The multi-purpose Bestie Valley Trail skirts Crystal Lake for a mile on the northern edge of the natural area while the Mary Margaret Johnson Trail, open only to foot traffic, heads inland from Mollineaux Road to views of Crystal Lake. Even though they are not connected, a short segment of Mollineaux Road allows you to combine the trails for an enjoyable bike-and-hike outing.

The Mary Margaret Johnson Trail was completed in 2011 to replace the old logging roads visitors were using when the natural area first opened. The foot trail dips and climbs as it follows the natural contours of the terrain for a round-trip hike of 1.3 miles.

Access and Information

The trailhead for the Mary Margaret Johnson Trail is posted along Mollineaux Road, which forms a loop off of M-115, 3 miles east of M-22 in Frankfort or 2 miles west of US-31 in Benzonia. There are no facilities or drinking water at the trailhead.

For more information, contact the Grand Traverse Regional Land Conservancy (231-929-7911; www.gtrlc.org).

On The Trail

From the trailhead, the Mary Margaret Johnson Trail enters the upland forest to skirt the edge of a wooded hollow. There's a bit of climbing here as you dip in and out of a small ravine before reaching a junction guarded by a pair of huge oak trees at *Mile 0.3*.

To the east (right), a loop continues to follow the rolling contour of the bluff and within a quarter mile reaches its edge, where there are views of Crystal Lake through the foliage. The trail skirts the bluff briefly, then heads inland, returning to the junction at **Mile 0.75**.

Head right. Within 100 yards the trail breaks out of the forest into a small opening on the edge of the lakeshore bluff where a bench has been placed. Below is the brilliantly blue water of Crystal Lake. The 9,854-acre lake is 8 miles long and has more than 20 miles of shoreline. The average depth of Crystal Lake is 70 feet but its deepest point is 165 feet, the reason its diverse fishery includes lake trout.

The sunset behind bluffs along Crystal Lake as seen from Railroad Point Natural Area (photo by Kathy Partin).

What makes the lake so beautiful to many are the ridges and bluffs that encircle it and were once home to a small downhill ski area. The bench in the natural area is perched on top of one of the highest at almost 700 feet, or 116 feet above Lake Michigan.

To return to the trailhead, backtrack the trail bypassing the loop along the way. You will reach the small parking area along Mollineaux Road in less than a half mile.

Elberta Dunes South
Natural Area

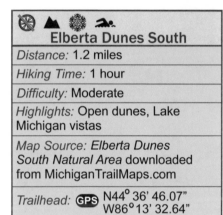

Elberta Dunes South
Distance: 1.2 miles
Hiking Time: 1 hour
Difficulty: Moderate
Highlights: Open dunes, Lake Michigan vistas
Map Source: Elberta Dunes South Natural Area downloaded from MichiganTrailMaps.com
Trailhead: GPS N44° 36' 46.07" W86° 13' 32.64"

Tiny Elberta, population 372, is located on a small peninsula, surrounded by Lake Michigan to the west, Betsie Lake to the north and Betsie River to the east. Anchoring the village to the south is a towering ridge that rises almost 260 feet above everything else.

A big dune in a little town overlooking a spectacular beach.

Long used by locals as a recreation area, the tract was purchased by the village of Elberta, with assistance from the Grand Traverse Regional Land Conservancy and a grant from the Michigan Natural Resources Trust Fund, in 2010. The following year Elberta Dunes South Natural Area was dedicated as a 58-acre preserve.

Squeezed between M-22 and Lake Michigan, Elberta Dunes South is not big nor is its trail system extensive, a mere half mile or so. But the area is spectacular. Its western boundary is 1,425 feet of Lake Michigan shoreline that leads to another 1.2 miles of undeveloped beach to the north. Between the wide beach and the state highway are fields, forested ridgelines and an 845-foot dune with slopes that exceed 60 percent.

Elberta Dunes South is both beautiful and rare. Almost three-quarters of the preserve has been classified as a Critical Dune Area by the State of Michigan. Within its boundaries is the federally-listed threatened Pitcher's Thistle and the Lake Huron Locust, a state-threatened insect, while endangered Piping Plovers use the shoreline for nesting.

Though a number of social trails crisscross the area, the preserve's only dedicated trail is well marked and easy to follow. But not especially easy to hike. The 0.6-mile, point-to-point trail climbs steeply in places until it reaches the crest of the dune to reward visitors with magnificent views. In the winter, it is an excellent destination for snowshoers.

Access and Information

Elberta Dunes South is posted along M-22 (also labeled Frankfort

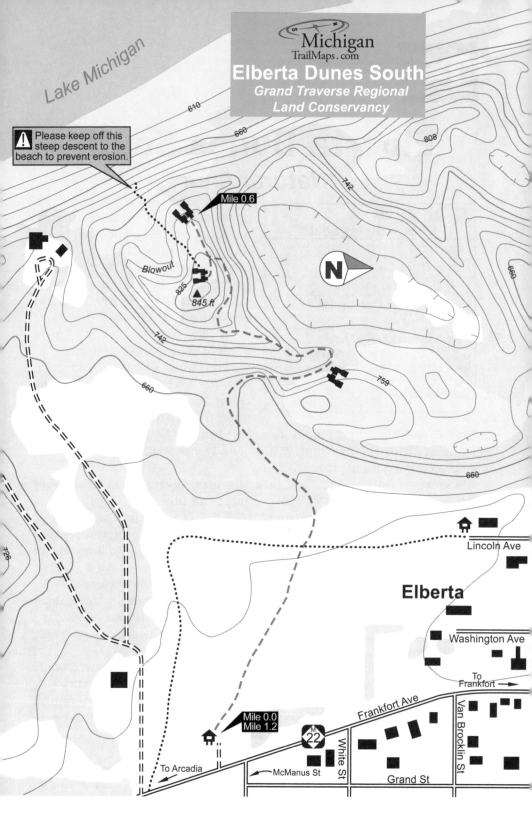

Lake Michigan

Michigan
TrailMaps.com
Elberta Dunes South
*Grand Traverse Regional
Land Conservancy*

⚠ Please keep off this
steep descent to the
beach to prevent erosion.

610

660

808

742

Mile 0.6

Blowout

825

845 ft

N

742

660

759

660

726

Lincoln Ave

Elberta

Washington Ave

To
Frankfort →

Frankfort Ave

Van Brocklin St

Mile 0.0
Mile 1.2

M22

White St

To Arcadia

McManus St

Grand St

Enjoying the view of Lake Michigan from Elberta Dunes South Natural Area.

Avenue) in Elberta, less than a mile south of where the state highway crosses the Betsie River. For more information, contact the Grand Traverse Regional Land Conservancy (231-929-7911; *www.gtrlc.org*).

On The Trail

Take note: There is no source of drinking water at the trailhead, with an uphill climb ahead. From the parking area, the trail heads west across a field as a mowed lane. After crossing another mowed lane, the trail from the Lincoln Avenue trailhead, you enter the woods and begin climbing.

The trail heads north and quickly reaches the edge of a grassy bowl where there is a view of the village in the distance. It then swings south into the woods and continues its ascent, following a narrow ridgeline that leads to the steepest climb of the hike. At **Mile 0.5** you pop out of the trees on the edge of a huge, open blowout facing Lake Michigan.

A trail to the west (right) continues a short distance to a small knob with views of the shoreline to the south. The trail to the east (left) climbs a

. higher for a different perspective of Lake Michigan and the surrounding dune country. At either, you can take a well-earned break and savor the scene below.

Leading down through the open bowl is another unofficial path. Please keep off this sensitive area and the steep slope to Lake Michigan to prevent erosion. Beach access is available at Elberta Beach to the North.

A Rare Thistle In The Dunes

Pitcher's Thistle (USFS photo).

In the 1820s Dr. Zina Pitcher, an army surgeon based at Fort Brady in Sault Ste. Marie, was also an accomplished botanist who loved to roam the wild areas of the Upper Peninsula. It was during one of these treks in the Grand Sable Dunes that Dr. Pitcher discovered a handsome, white-flowered thistle he had never seen before. Nor had anybody else and eventually the plant was named in his honor; Pitcher's thistle.

This rare plant grows nowhere else in the world except among open, wind-blown coastal dunes of Lake Michigan, Lake Huron and Lake Superior. Pitcher's thistle can withstand the desert-like environment because its roots are capable of penetrating more than 6 feet of sand in search of moisture. The dense, silvery hairs covering its leaves and stem also aid the plant in water retention while reflecting the sun's strongest rays.

Pitcher's thistle can reach a height of more than 3 feet while its leaves, divide into narrow, spine-tipped segments, can grow to a foot in length. Its prickly flower heads, guarded by spines, bloom from June to September and range in color from creamy white to slightly pinkish. Pitcher's thistle is monocarpic. Juvenile plants take five to eight years to mature before flowering and adult plants die after flowering once and setting seed.

Today the thistle is listed as a threatened species by the federal government and the state of Michigan due to a rapid loss of its dune habitat. Most of the erosion is caused by increased foot and vehicle traffic in foredune areas and along shorelines. You can help save the Pitcher's thistle by learning to recognize the plant and then keep an eye out for it when hiking in dune country.

Sleeping Bear Dunes National Lakeshore

Hikers return from Lake Michigan along the Old Indian Trail.

12

Old Indian Trail

Old Indian Trail	
Distance: 3.2 miles	
Hiking Time: 2 hours	
Difficulty: Easy	
Highlights: Lake Michigan beach, Ghost forest, Coastal dunes	
Map Source: Old Indian Trail from from MichiganTrailMaps.com or Sleeping Bear Dunes National Lakeshore at www.nps.gov/slbe	
Trailhead: GPS	N44° 42' 10.88" W86° 11' 24.31"

Anchoring the southern end of Sleeping Bear Dunes National Lakeshore in Benzie County is Old Indian Trail, a route that originally was used by Native Americans to access their fish camps along Lake Michigan. Although today Old Indian attracts less attention than any other trail in the park, it still provides access to a beautiful beach and is a rare escape from the summer crowds encountered elsewhere in this popular park.

Old Indian is a pair of trails that form a loop, merging a quarter mile from the shoreline. Most of the trail dips and climbs through a forest of red and white pines or a mix of hemlocks, maples and oaks. It also breaks out occasionally in small grassy meadows and marshes. Closer to Lake Michigan is a series of low dunes covered with grasses and shrubs bordering a wide, sandy beach.

Following the perimeter of the loops out to the beach and back would be a 3.2-mile, one- to two-hour trek. Overall, Old Indian is an easy walk along a wide path. The Black Arrow Loop is by far the more interesting of the two as it dips and climbs a series of old beach dunes now forested and is the hike described below.

The trail is also a popular area for Nordic skiers. The Green Arrow Loop, rated easy for beginners, is relatively flat with only a couple of gentle slopes. Black Arrow is rated intermediate and has one steep downhill section in the northeast corner of the loop.

Access and Information

From the Philip Hart Visitor Center in Empire, head south on M-22 for 12 miles and look for the entrance to the trailhead parking lot, which is posted on the north (right) side of the road. If heading north from Frankfort, follow M-22 and look for the posted entrance just beyond Sutter Road.

The trail is open year-round and visitors are required to have a weekly vehicle entrance permit, an annual park pass or a per-person pass if on foot, bicycle or motorcycle. Passes can be purchased at an automated pay station

Michigan
TrailMaps.com

Old Indian Trail
Sleeping Bear Dunes
National Lakeshore

Lake Michigan

Coastal Dunes

Mile 1.8

594

627

Mile 1.5

Black Arrow Loop

Mile 2.1

610

Unofficial Trail

Green Arrow Loop

Mile 0.3

Green Arrow Loop

Sutter Rd

Mile 0.0
Mile 3.2

M22

To Emp

Long
Lake

660

N

M22

To Frankfort

742

A ghost forest, trees that have died from migrating dunes, along the Old Indian Trail.

at the trailhead or from the Philip Hart Visitor Center (231-326-5134; www.
nps.gov/slbe) in Empire.

On The Trail

Within the parking area is a display sign and map box along with a vault
toilet but no source of drinking water. From the information kiosk, a foot
path departs into a mix of hemlocks, maples and oaks and for the most part
remains in the forest, keeping you cool even on the hottest summer day.

You quickly pass the posted junction with the return of the Green Arrow
Loop from the west (left). Continue north and the next junction is reached
in a third of a mile. Stay north at this junction to follow the Black Arrow
Loop. This route is hilly enough to be marked by black triangles indicating
an "Advanced" trail for skiers. For the next mile, you hike over a series of
low dunes, forested in mixed hardwoods (maple, beech, oak) and pines. You

You're In Cougar Country

Old Indian has one of the most unusual warning signs found at any trailhead in Michigan: *You Are A Visitor In Cougar Habitat.*

It was along this trail that several cougar sightings were reported and resulted in the NPS posting the sign here and elsewhere in the park. The trailhead sign goes on to inform visitors that seeing a cougar can be a thrilling experience but if you do encounter one you should remain calm and not run. If approached, wave your arms and throw sticks and rocks. If attacked, fight back aggressively.

What a way to spice up a hike to the beach.

Thought to be extinct in Michigan by 1900, cougar sightings have sparked a controversy as to whether there is now a breeding population in the state. The large cats, also referred to as mountain lions, range in size from 80 to 200 pounds and are seven to nine feet long from the nose to the tip of the tail. They are usually tan or brown with black-tipped ears and tail, and whitetail deer, not beach bunnies, is their chief prey. In the past century, only 13 people have been killed by cougars in North America.

remain in the woods except when the trail descends to a marsh or pond.

At **Mile 1.2**, you pass a spot where open dunes are migrating south into the forest, sand pouring down between the trees. From here, it's a third of a mile to the posted junction where you head north (right) to the beach. From the junction you immediately climb a dune, the steepest of the hike, and from the top enjoy a sweeping view of Lake Michigan. Blue tipped posts then lead you past a ghost forest and through open dunes before ending at the shoreline, a quarter mile from the junction.

This is a scenic spot, even though a couple of cottages are visible to the west. To the east, you view nothing but the wide expanse of low beach dunes along Platte Bay, while in the distance is the famous Sleeping Bear Dune. Out in the lake are North and South Manitou islands, with South Manitou's perched dunes along its west side clearly visible. The beach is usually 20 to 30 feet wide, depending on the lake level, and you can walk the length of it to the mouth of Platte River, a trek of more than 3 miles.

To return, backtrack a quarter mile to the beach junction and this time head southeast along the Green Arrow Loop. The level route quickly passes a junction to the northern leg of the Green Arrow Loop and at **Mile 2.4** green "Easy" triangles mark the southern leg of the loop. Head east (left) along this route and avoid the unmarked trail that continues to the south.

The final leg is 0.75 miles long and relatively flat. It traverses ancient beach dunes that mark the former Lake Michigan shoreline, when the water level was considerably higher in the early postglacial era. At one point, you pass through an impressive stand of beech, with one huge tree right next to the trail. Eventually, you arrive at the first junction you passed from the trailhead. Head south (right) to quickly reach the parking lot at **Mile 3.2**.

13

Platte Plains Trail

Platte Plains Trail
▲ ❄ ⛺ 🚲 ▲ 🚣 🚰
Distance: 7.2 miles
Hiking Time: 3-5 hours
Difficulty: Easy
Highlights: Walk-in campsites, Lake Michigan beaches,
Map Source: Platte Plains Trail from MichiganTrailMaps.com or Sleeping Bear Dunes National Lakeshore at www.nps.gov/slbe
Trailhead: GPS N44° 43' 11.36" W86°7' 2.54"

Stretched out along serene Platte Bay is Platte Plains. This slice of the Sleeping Bear Dunes National Lakeshore offers outstanding coastal scenery, some of the finest beaches in Michigan and a trail system and terrain that is as tranquil as the bay is at sunset on a quiet evening.

Most of Platte Plains is a level to gently rolling landscape forested in oak, aspen and pines. It's boxed in by Lake Michigan to the west, Platte River to the south, Otter Creek and Otter Lake to the north and M-22 to the east and south. The area is crisscrossed by a network of old logging roads with one trail following the bed of a narrow gauge railroad track once used to haul timber to Lake Michigan.

The plains are a series of low dunes. Many were ancient shorelines left high and dry after the glaciers retreated and Lake Michigan levels changed. Others are beach dunes formed by prevailing westerly winds that pushed the sand inland. At the north end of the plains are the Aral Dunes, topping 100 feet in height. The rest of the dunes are considerably smaller. The steepest climbs hikers will face are only 50 to 60 feet in elevation.

The most beautiful aspect of the area is the shoreline, with a wide, sandy beach lined by low, windswept dunes and framed in to the north by the towering Empire Bluffs. It's hard to argue with those who say this is the finest beach and shoreline setting in Michigan.

Platte Plains Trail is a 15-mile network of trails with four trailheads and a walk-in campground. The northern section of the trail system – Otter Creek, Otter Lake and Bass Lake, with trailheads on Trail's End Road and Esch Road – is covered as a separate hike (page 73). The hike described here is a scenic route that begins at Platte River Campground, includes the White Pine Backcountry Campground and is referred to as the Lasso Loop.

This loop is a 7.2-mile trek, with the walk-in campground reached in 2.8 miles. Many undertake this trail as a day hike; for others it is an ideal choice for their first backpacking experience with its easy terrain and ban on mountain bikes. Surprisingly, for a park as overrun as Sleeping Bear Dunes can be in the summer, the demand for campsites at White Pine is moderately

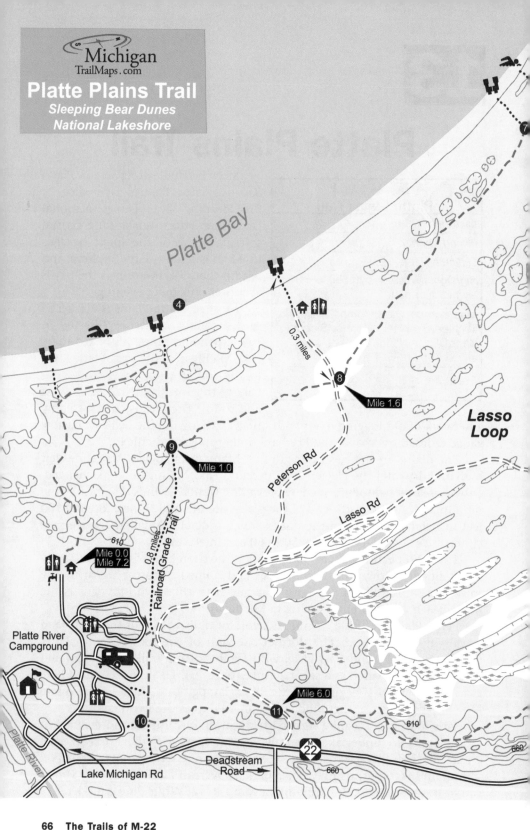

Michigan TrailMaps.com

Platte Plains Trail
Sleeping Bear Dunes National Lakeshore

Platte Bay

4

0.3 miles

8
Mile 1.6

Lasso Loop

9
Mile 1.0

Peterson Rd

Lasso Rd

610

Mile 0.0
Mile 7.2

0.8 miles

Railroad Grade Trail

Platte River
Campground

Mile 6.0

11

10

M-22

Platte River

Lake Michigan Rd

Deadstream Road →

610

660

660

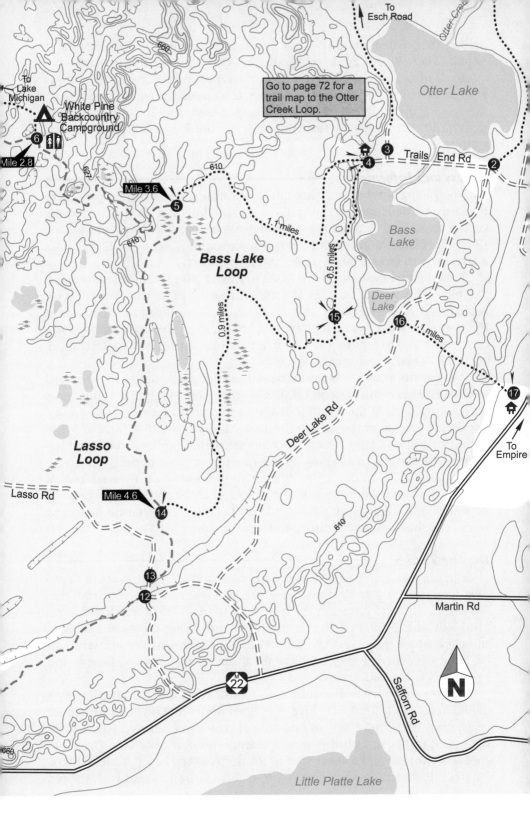

To
Esch Road

To
Lake
Michigan

Otter Lake

White Pine
Backcountry
Campground

6

Mile 2.8

660

610

Mile 3.6

5

Go to page 72 for a
trail map to the Otter
Creek Loop.

3

4

Trails End Rd

2

1.1 miles

Bass
Lake

0.5 miles

Bass Lake
Loop

Deer
Lake

15

16

1.1 miles

0.9 miles

17

Lasso
Loop

Deer Lake Rd

To
Empire

Lasso Rd

Mile 4.6

14

610

13

12

Martin Rd

M22

Saffron Rd

N

660

Little Platte Lake

light. Often, when there is a line of campers waiting for an opening at popular Platte River Campground, sites at White Pine are still available.

If planning to spend a night in the backcountry, pack in a water filter along with food, tent, sleeping bag, and other equipment. There's a community fire ring in the campground, but cooking is best done on a backpacker's stove. And don't forget the bathing suit; the beaches near White Pine are scenic and uncrowded.

Access and Information

The hiking season runs through the typical spring-to-fall period, with the heaviest demand for the walk-in sites in July and August, especially on the weekends. October brings in the spectacular fall colors and by late December Platte Plains, with its own winter trailhead off of M-22, becomes a favorite with cross-country skiers and snowshoers.

From Empire, head south on M-22 to reach Platte River Campground in 9.5 miles. This facility features 179 sites, including those with hook-ups for recreational vehicles and 25 walk-in sites that are secluded in the woods at the west end. There is also a picnic area, water, showers and restrooms. You can reserve a site through the national park reservation system Recreation. gov (877-444-6777; *www.recreation.gov*).

Along with a vehicle permit required to park at the trailhead, you need to obtain a backcountry permit if planning to spend a night at White Pine. Both are available at the Philip Hart Visitor Center (231-326-5134; *www.nps. gov/slbe*) in Empire or the Ranger Contact Station (231-326-4700, ext. 5029) at the Platte River Campground. Backcountry permits are available on a first-come-first-serve basis and allow up to two tents and four persons per site.

An alternative trailhead to White Pine is located at the west end of Peterson Road, where there is parking, a vault toilet and beach access but no source of drinking water. Nearby Lasso Loop crosses Peterson Road and reaches the backcountry campground in 1.2 miles.

On The Trail

Parking is available near the ranger contact station or the Walk-in Camp Area loop, where a trail, marked by blue triangles, departs into the pine forest and is easy to follow in the hilly terrain. In less than a half mile, you break out of the trees and enter the low dunes along the Lake Michigan shoreline where many quickly discover how tiring hiking on soft sand can be. Nearby is a locator map, and straight ahead are the cool lake breezes and a scenic view of the beach.

To the east (right) is the sandy path to post No. 9 and the junction with the Railroad Grade Trail. You hike over open dunes and through patches of beach grass. Here and there an odd pine or cottonwood thrives, but mostly the trail is in the sun until it swings sharply south at *Mile 0.8*. The views are excellent here and a short spur heads north to the beach. In less than a quarter mile to the south is post No. 9, where the trail merges with the old

A hiker on the spur to Lake Michigan along the Platte Plains Trail.

A backpacker sets up camp at the White Pine Backcountry Campground.

railroad grade.

You don't have to be a train buff to envision a line running along the wide and level path. The narrow-gauge line was built in the 19th century between Edgewater, a logging town on the west end of Platte Lake, to docks on Lake Michigan, where ships were loaded with lumber destined for Chicago.

The old grade heads south toward M-22, while Lasso Loop continues east (left) at post No. 9. Marked by green (easy) triangles, the trail enters a forest for more solid footing than the dunes and at **Mile 1.6** breaks out in a grassy clearing to arrive at Peterson Road. A short walk to the left on the dirt road leads to a parking area, vault toilet, another stretch of beautiful beach, and sweeping views of the bay.

Northeast of Peterson Road, the trail remains in the lightly forested area before entering a thicker stand of oak and pine. At **Mile 2.6** is post No. 7, the junction with another access spur to the lake. The views along the spur are stunning – the entire bay along with the famous Sleeping Bear Dunes lies to the north and South Manitou Island on the horizon. The main trail swings east from post No. 7 and at **Mile 2.8** reaches post No. 6, marking White Pine Backcountry Campground.

White Pine is located in a narrow ravine, with wooded ridges running along both sides of the secluded sites. The campground has a vault toilet and a community fire ring but no source of drinking water. There is no view of the lake from the campground, but near site No. 6 a path wanders west to quickly reach an area of windblown dunes. From the perch of the highest one, you are rewarded with an immense view of the mainland dunes and South Manitou Island. The Lake Michigan beach, with its clear waters and sandy bottom, is just another dune or two away. Return in the evening to watch the sun melt into Lake Michigan. What more could you ask for in a campsite?

From the campground, the loop continues due east. The triangles change color, from green (easy) to black (advanced). It's rated primarily for skiers, but hikers will also notice the walking is a little more strenuous. The approaching ridges and hills are ancient shoreline sand dunes that mark the position of Lake Michigan after each glacial ice melt. The steepest climb is within a quarter mile of post No. 6, and after topping off, the trail follows the crest of the ridge around a marshy pond. You descend, climb again to skirt another pond, and then drop quickly to the base of that dune. The trail levels out somewhat, winds through an impressive stand of pines, and at **Mile 3.6** comes to post No. 5 and the junction with Bass Lake Loop.

To the north (left) is the 1.1-mile spur to post No. 4, marking Trail's End Road trailhead (see Otter Creek Loop page 73). Lasso Loop continues south (right) along a level stretch for another interesting change of scenery. On one side of the path are towering pines with a thick understory of ferns while on the other side is a series of marshes filled with cattails. The largest marsh is seen at **Mile 4** and often in June wild irises can be spotted from the trail. Other marshes follow for almost the entire 1.1-mile stretch.

Post No. 14 is reached at **Mile 4.6**, where Lasso Loop heads right. Within a third of a mile you break out at Lasso Road at post No. 13 and follow the two-track briefly before veering off to the west at post No. 12, a spot that is occasionally missed by hikers who continue to follow the dirt road.

The forested terrain remains level for the next mile and then the trail resumes skirting ancient lakeshore dunes. At one point, there are forested ridges on both sides of the path. After swinging so close to M-22 that on a busy summer weekend you can hear the traffic, the trail climbs a ridge to wind past more marshy areas. The open wetlands and meadows remain visible until you drop back down into the forest and at **Mile 6** cross Peterson Road a second time.

On the other side of the road, the trail swings north and eventually merges with the Railroad Grade Trail. Turn right here and follow the old line. Spurs to the campground quickly appear, with one to Loop 2 posted. You emerge in that loop next to campsite No. 217 and follow the campground road to wherever you parked your vehicle.

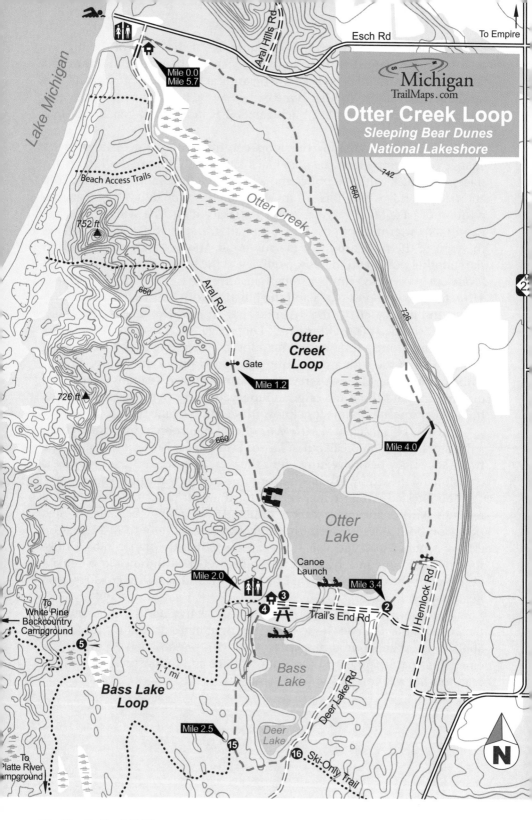

Lake Michigan

Esch Rd

To Empire

Aral Hills Rd

Michigan
TrailMaps.com

Otter Creek Loop
Sleeping Bear Dunes
National Lakeshore

Mile 0.0
Mile 5.7

Beach Access Trails

Otter Creek

752 ft

Aral Rd

660

660

742

660

726

Otter Creek Loop

Gate
Mile 1.2

726 ft

Mile 4.0

Otter Lake

Canoe Launch

Mile 2.0

Mile 3.4

3

2

4

Hemlock Rd

To White Pine Backcountry Campground

Trail's End Rd

5

1.1 mi

Bass Lake Loop

Bass Lake

Deer Lake

Deer Lake Rd

To Platte River Campground

Mile 2.5

15

16

Ski-Only Trail

N

Otter Creek Loop

Otter Creek Loop
A ❄ ⊕ 🐟 🏕 🦆
Distance: 5.7 miles
Hiking Time: 2-3 hours
Difficulty: Moderate
Highlights: Otter Creek, Inland lakes, Lake Michigan beaches
Map Source: Otter Creek Loop from MichiganTrailMaps.com or Platte Plains Trail from Sleeping Bear Dunes National Lakeshore at www.nps.gov/slbe
Trailhead: GPS N44° 45" 44.07" W86° 4' 24.66"

In 1880, the mouth of Otter Creek became the site of Aral, a bustling logging town of more than 100 residents that included a schoolhouse, company store, a two-story lumber mill and an extensive wharf where freshly milled timber was loaded onto ships and steam barges for the lumber-starved cities of the Great Plains. When the forests disappeared by 1911, so did Aral — today, the only trace of the town is a set of dock pilings poking out of Lake Michigan.

In an ironic twist, the beaches south of Otter Creek are now some of the most isolated in Sleeping Bear Dunes National Lakeshore, prompting so many naturists and clothing-optional swimmers to visit the area that the park has posted this sign along Otter Creek Loop:

Notice: Pubic Nudity is Prohibited in Michigan. KEEP YOUR SWIMSUIT ON!

From lumberjacks to skinny-dippers to some of the best birding in the area, Otter Creek Loop is one of the most unusual trails in Sleeping Bear Dunes.

Officially, Otter Creek is a 4.6-mile loop and part of the Platte Plains Trail, a nearly 15-mile network that stretches from the Platte River Campground to Esch Road and includes four trailheads, a walk-in campground and 4 miles of incredibly beautiful beach along Platte Bay. But while Otter Creek is connected with Bass Lake Loop and thus Lasso Loop (see page 65), for most hikers it's a distinct outing on its own.

Otter Creek is described here as a 5.7-mile trek that combines the trail, a segment of Bass Lake Loop and portions of Aral and Deer Lake Roads, narrow, seasonal two-tracks. This route leads along both sides of the creek as well as the shorelines of three pristine lakes: Otter, Bass and Deer.

For many, the appeal of Otter Creek Loop is neither remote beaches nor its link to Michigan's logging era but the possibility of viewing wildlife, particularly birds. The mix of woodlands, dunes, shoreline and shrub-scrub wetlands makes the area one of the best in the national lakeshore for birding. Among the birds that may be encountered are bald eagles, Sandhill cranes, herons, rails and a variety of waterfowl that frequent the creek.

Otter Creek just upstream from where it flows into Lake Michigan.

In late May, Otter Creek is an excellent place to see migrating warblers, while in the summer scarlet tanagers and Baltimore orioles can be spotted in the woods along the roads and two-tracks.

Access and Information

From Empire, head south on M-22 for 3.8 miles and then west on Esch Road for 1.3 miles. The road ends at a beach access parking area that includes a vault toilet. Just before the beach access is Aral Road, a two-track that heads south and in 100 yards passes the Otter Creek Loop trailhead and post No. 1.

A vehicle permit is required to park at the trailhead and is available at the Philip Hart Visitor Center (231-326-5134; *www.nps.gov/slbe*) in Empire or the Platte River Campground Ranger Station (231-326-4700, ext. 5029).

On The Trail

The first leg of Otter Creek Loop is Aral Road, a narrow two-track that is followed for more than a mile and makes for easy hiking. The road begins by crossing a vehicle bridge over Otter Creek and then climbs above it, allowing you to spot wildlife that may be gathering on the wetlands below. Along the way, two beach access trails, posted with keep-your-swimsuit-on signs, are passed before Aral Road swings out of view of the creek at **Mile 0.5**.

A third beach access trail is passed and then at **Mile 1.2** a gate prevents vehicles from traveling any further. Beyond the gate, a wide foot path replaces the old two-track and continues south into the pine-hardwood forest where in less than a half mile it reaches the northwest corner of Otter Lake. This scenic spot is posted and makes for a great place to relax if you're not in a hurry. The trail briefly skirts the shoreline and then passes one of the few private cabins on Otter Lake, using its access road to arrive at Trail's End Road and the Bass Lake Loop Trailhead at *Mile 2*.

The day-use area of Bass Lake includes vault toilets, picnic tables, a fishing pier and a canoe launch. At the trailhead, post No. 4, one trail heads west for the White Pine Backcountry Campground on the Lasso Loop. The other heads south for post No. 15. Go south and you'll skirt the scenic lake and then climb above it for a view of the entire body of water. Post No. 15 is reached at *Mile 2.5* and marks the junction of the spur to the winter-only Ski Trailhead on M-22.

In less than a quarter mile east on the ski trail spur, you break out at the south end of Deer Lake, the smallest of the three. The trail skirts it briefly, allowing you to search for wildlife, particularly beavers and otters, before arriving at post No. 16 on Deer Lake Road at *Mile 2.9*. The ski trail spur continues east, while heading north is Deer Lake Road, another seasonal two-track open to vehicles. There are more views of Deer Lake and then Bass Lake before returning to Trail's End Road, marked by post No. 2 at *Mile 3.4*.

On the north side, the trail passes another private residence on Otter Lake and then follows Hemlock Road to a second gate, this one blocking vehicles from continuing onto Otter Creek Loop from the two-track. Otter Creek Loop is now a level foot path that heads north through the forest and small meadows and reaches a foot bridge at *Mile 4*. Beyond the stream you skirt the base of a steep wooded dune that at times rises more than 110 feet.

The imposing bluff remains for a while before the trail swings west near Otter Creek at *Mile 4.8* and then enters an impressive stand of cedar. Eventually, a red pine plantation takes over and at *Mile 5.7* you pop out of the pines at post No. 1 and the Otter Creek Loop trailhead on Aral Road.

Fishing the Lakes of Platte Plains

The inland lakes of Platte Plains make for one of the best fishing adventures in Sleeping Bear Dunes National Lakeshore. All three are non-motorized and only Otter Lake has a few cottages by it. Early in the morning or at dusk, times when anglers generally do best, a range of wildlife, from bald eagles to otters, can be encountered.

Canoes and fishing kayaks work best on the larger Otter Lake and can be launched from an unimproved ramp off Trail's End Road on the south side of the lake. Float tubes also work well in the other two lakes, particularly Deer Lake. At Bass Lake, facilities include a handicap-accessible canoe launch and a fishing pier.

Deer Lake is the most difficult to reach and involves following often badly-rutted Deer Lake Road 0.6 mile south from Trail's End Road and then carrying your boat in. A channel connects Bass Lake with Deer Lake and at one time anglers could paddle from one to the next. But beavers and their lodges in have eliminated that easy access to Deer Lake.

All three lakes are warm-water fisheries with anglers targeting smallmouth bass, a variety of panfish and northern pike.

The view from the end of the Empire Bluff Trail.

Empire Bluff Trail

Empire Bluff Trail

Distance: 1.5 miles	
Hiking Time: 1 hour	
Difficulty: Moderate	
Highlights: Scenic vistas of Lake Michigan	
Map Source: Empire Bluff Trail from MichiganTrailMaps.com or Sleeping Bear Dunes National Lakeshore at www.nps.gov/slbe	
Trailhead: **GPS**	N44° 47' 56.97" W86°3' 30.78"

Few trails in Sleeping Bear Dunes National Lakeshore, or in Michigan for that matter, lead to a more spectacular view than this short path to the edge of Empire Bluff.

The bluff rises to 1,106 feet, or more than 500 feet above the sandy shoreline of Lake Michigan, and skirting its steep slope at the end of the trail becomes a lofty perch to view a large portion of the national lakeshore. Add six interpretive posts and an accompanying brochure that explains the natural and geological history of the area, and you have one of the best short hikes in the state.

The round trip is only 1.5 miles, but is rated moderate due to the amount of climbing involved. Watch out for poison ivy, prevalent in the open areas along the trail, and refrain from descending the sandy bluffs at the end since it's a longer climb back up than most people realize and hastens erosion.

The trail is open year-round and is a far better trek on snowshoes than on Nordic skis, even for those with backcountry skis. Mountain biking is not allowed.

Empire Bluff makes for an excellent family hike and can be done by most people in less than an hour. Pack along a lunch and enjoy refueling to a fantastic view that would rival any of Michigan's finest restaurants. Better yet, bring a flashlight and arrive near dusk on a clear evening for a sunset second to none.

Access and Information

From the Philip Hart Visitor Center on the corner of M-22 and M-72 in Empire, head south on M-22 for 1.7 miles and then west (right) on Wilco Road. Within a mile the trailhead is on the left.

An annual or weekly vehicle permit is required to enter the national lakeshore and can be purchased from the Philip Hart Visitor Center on the corner of M-22 and M-72 in Empire or from a self-registration tube at the trailhead. For more information contact the Philip Hart Visitor Center (231-326-5134; *www.nps.gov/slbe*).

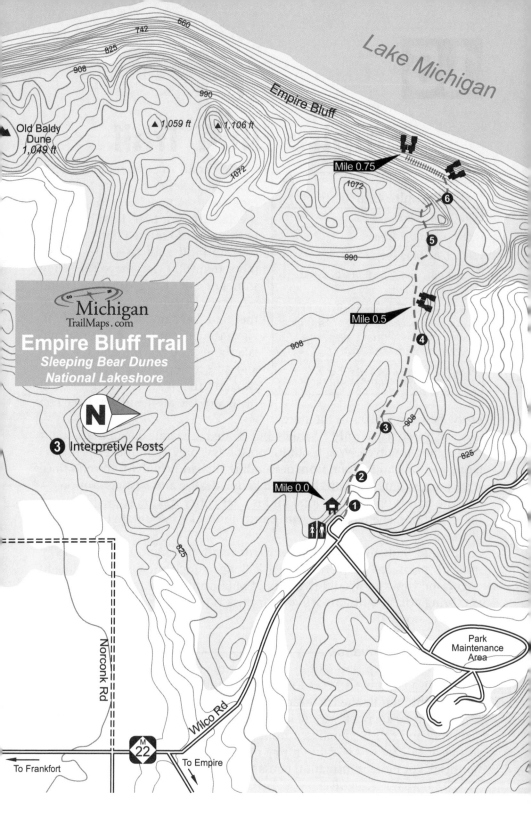

Lake Michigan

Empire Bluff

742
660
825
908
990
Old Baldy Dune 1,049 ft
▲ 1,059 ft
▲ 1,106 ft
1072

Mile 0.75

6

1072

5

990

Michigan
TrailMaps.com

Empire Bluff Trail
*Sleeping Bear Dunes
National Lakeshore*

Mile 0.5

4

N

3 Interpretive Posts

908

3

908

825

2

Mile 0.0

1

825

Park
Maintenance
Area

Norconk Rd

Wilco Rd

M 22

To Frankfort

To Empire

The first viewing point along the Empire Bluff Trail.

On The Trail

At the Wilco Road trailhead there is a small parking area with a display sign, map box and a vault toilet but no drinking water.

The trail begins with an immediate climb past post No. 1, which marks an out-of-place boulder. Glaciers that picked up rocks and soil in Canada and the Upper Peninsula retreated here 11,800 years ago, leaving debris behind as bluffs, hills, and out-of-place boulders known as erratics. You move into a beech-maple forest that borders a former farm field and at post No. 2 can examine some old farm equipment left behind from the 1940s.

Another climb brings you to the crest of a ridge where the trail levels out, passes two more posts and at **Mile 0.5** arrives at the first panoramic view of the hike. Here you can sit on a bench and gaze at the Lake Michigan shoreline to the north.

Eventually, you descend off the ridge, bottom out at post No. 5 and then make the final climb to post No. 6, where you break out of the forest to witness a spectacular panorama framed by dune grass, weathered trees and often a blue sky.

It's a breathtaking sight for anybody who didn't envision such a reward at the end of such a short walk. Almost 300 feet above the lake, you can view Platte Bay to the south and the Sleeping Bear Bluffs to the north, with the famous Sleeping Bear Dune itself appearing as a small hill on top of the high, sandy ridge. Seven miles out on the horizon is South Manitou Island.

At this point, the trail swings south and follows a boardwalk along the bluffs for 500 feet to an observation area with a series of benches. You might have walked less than a mile but with such a splendid view, you could rest here for hours.

Hikers trek through open dunes near the Cottonwood Trail.

16

Cottonwood Trail

𝗄 ⊛ ▲ 🎋 🏕
Cottonwood Trail
Distance: 1.7 miles
Hiking Time: 1 hour
Difficulty: Moderate
Highlights: Scenic vistas of Dune Climb and Glen Lake
Map Source: Cottonwood Trail from MichiganTrailMaps.com or Sleeping Bear Dunes National Lakeshore at www.nps.gov/slbe
Trailhead: **GPS** N44° 52' 24.52" W86° 3' 7.26"

Pierce Stocking Scenic Drive is a 7.4-mile, one-way loop within national lakeshore that is often called "the slowest, shortest, but most scenic stretch of pavement in the state."

The speed limit on the single-lane road is only 15 miles per hour as it passes four stunning overlooks that include the park's famous perched dunes, Lake Michigan and Glen Lake. So spectacular is the scenery that most people don't want to leave the road or overlooks, so they pass up the Cottonwood Trail that departs Pierce Stocking Scenic Drive at stop No. 4.

That's a shame.

Cottonwood Trail is worthy of having a trailhead along Scenic Drive, featuring several dramatic viewing points of its own. The 1.7-mile loop winds through the perched dunes above the Dune Climb and provides a close look at the beauty of these shifting hills of open sand as well as the vegetation such as bearberry, buffaloberry, beachgrass and cottonwoods that are slowly stabilizing the dunes.

Cottonwood is an interpretive trail with nine posts that correspond to a self-guided brochure available at the trailhead or can be downloaded from *www.MichiganTrailMaps.com*. The brochure describes the plant life and geology of the area and explains why the mounds of advancing sand in this ever-changing land are so special and fragile.

The rolling dunes that surround the trail are part of Sleeping Bear Plateau, a 4-square-mile highland that rises more than 400 feet above Lake Michigan and is covered with a veneer of perched dunes. The price hikers pay for this unusual scenery is that much of the trail, particularly the first half, is hilly and through loose sand. Sandy slopes can be tiring, the reason this loop of less than 2 miles is rated moderate in difficulty.

Access and Information

From the Philip Hart Visitor Center (231-326-5134; *www.nps.gov/slbe*) in Empire, head north on M-22, veer left on M-109 and in 3 miles is the posted entrance to Pierce Stocking Scenic Drive. Follow the one-way road 2.3 miles

Admiring the view of Glen Lake from the Cottonwood Trail.

to post No. 4, marking the Dune Overlook. The Cottonwood Trail has its own parking area next to the often-busy Dune Overlook parking area. Also nearby is Picnic Mountain with drinking water, toilets and picnic tables.

The drive is open from 9 a.m. until sunset May through mid-November and requires a park entry permit that can be purchased at the Pierce Stocking contact station or from the visitor center.

On The Trail

There is no drinking water at the trailhead and even along this short trail you can get thirsty fast. Water is available at Picnic Mountain. From the information kiosk, Cottonwood Trail descends as a boardwalk at first, quickly passing three posts, one of them warning about poison ivy. In less than a quarter mile you reach the junction of the return trail and head right.

At this point, the trail skirts a huge blowout where the prevailing southwest winds carved out a smooth bowl-like depression. Its concave windward side is too tempting for some hikers not to scramble up it. Beyond post No. 5 you begin a steady climb and at *Mile 0.5* top off on a small sand-and-grassy knoll at 888 feet in elevation. The view is magnificent and includes Lake Michigan off in the distance along with Pyramid Point and the Manitou Islands. Almost 300 feet below to the east is Glen Lake.

For the next quarter mile you follow a sandy ridge of the dune and enjoy the wonderful views along it before climbing to a patch of cottonwoods at *Mile 0.75*, where post No. 7 and two benches are located. As good as the views have been, this one is the best. All around is a stunning panorama that includes open dunes, Lake Michigan, inland lakes, historic farms and faded red barns. Almost directly below is the park's famous Dune Climb — climbers will look like ants scurrying up the steep slope of sand. It would be easy at this point to descend to the Dune Climb picnic area or to the start of the Dunes Trail (see page 91).

Cottonwood Trail then heads west, descending off this high point to post No. 8 before swinging south for a return to the trailhead. Post No. 9, noting a rare stand of paper birch not normally seen in dune country, is reached at *Mile 1.1* and the junction is less than a half mile from there.

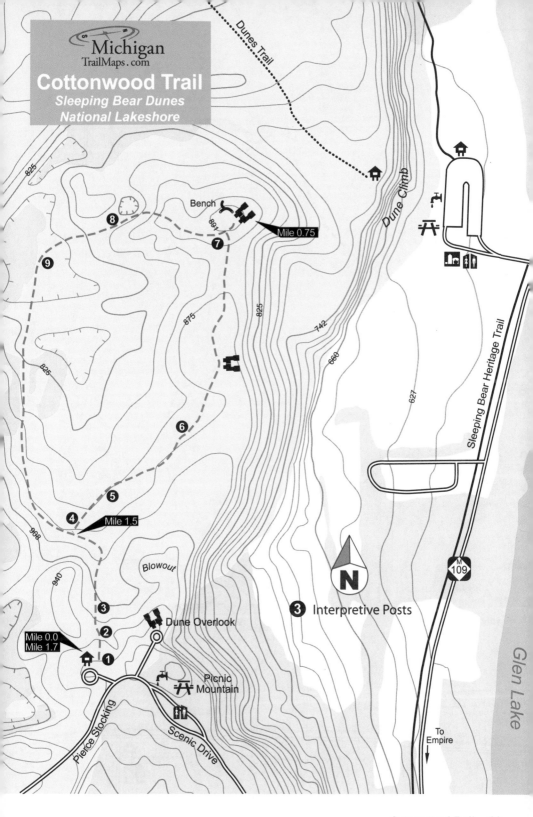

Michigan
TrailMaps.com

Cottonwood Trail
Sleeping Bear Dunes
National Lakeshore

Dunes Trail

Dune Climb

Bench

Mile 0.75

7

8

9

825

875

825

742

660

627

Sleeping Bear Heritage Trail

6

5

4 Mile 1.5

908

Blowout

940

N

M 109

3 Interpretive Posts

3

2

Dune Overlook

Mile 0.0
Mile 1.7

1

Picnic
Mountain

Pierce Stocking

Scenic Drive

To
Empire

Glen Lake

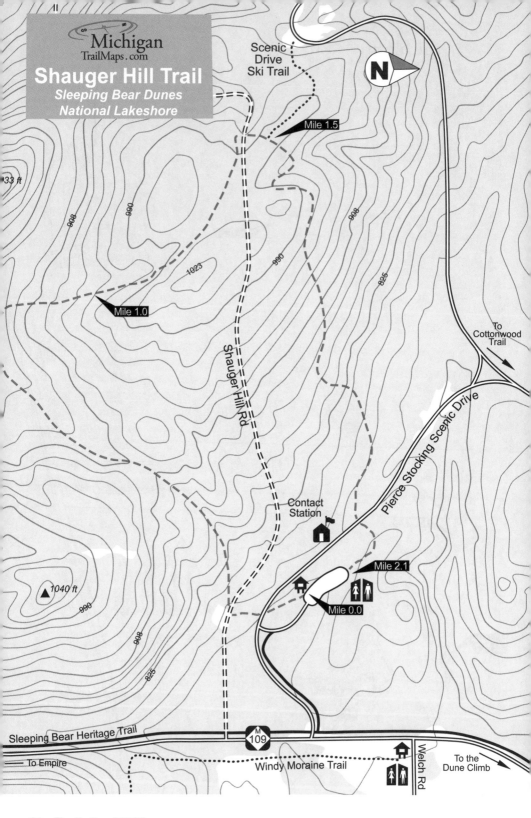

Shauger Hill Trail

Sleeping Bear Dunes National Lakeshore

Michigan
TrailMaps.com

N

Scenic Drive Ski Trail

Mile 1.5

Mile 1.0

33 ft

990

908

1023

990

998

825

Shauger Hill Rd

To Cottonwood Trail

Pierce Stocking Scenic Drive

Contact Station

Mile 2.1

Mile 0.0

1040 ft

990

908

825

Sleeping Bear Heritage Trail

M 109

To Empire

Windy Moraine Trail

Welch Rd

To the Dune Climb

17

Shauger Hill Trail

Shauger Hill Trail

Distance: 2.1 miles
Hiking Time: 1 hour
Difficulty: Moderate
Highlights: Hardwood forested ridges, Fall colors
Map Source: Shauger Hill Trail from MichiganTrailMaps.com or Sleeping Bear Dunes National Lakeshore at www.nps.gov/slbe
Trailhead: **GPS** N44° 51' 11.04" W86° 2' 11.88"

Most people who stop along Pierce Stocking Scenic Drive in Sleeping Bear Dunes National Lakeshore do so to enjoy the spectacular overlooks of Glen Lake or Lake Michigan, have a picnic or hike the Cottonwood Trail. But the 7.4-mile scenic road also provides access to a second trail that receives light usage even during the peak of the summer season.

Shauger Hill Trail is a wooded 2.1-mile loop with a trailhead and parking area near the contact station at the beginning of Scenic Drive. The hilly trail passes through a climax beech-maple forest, red pine plantations and a few small clearings and twice crosses Shauger Hill Road as well as Pierce Stocking Drive.

In the spring, it's an excellent trail for wildflowers and morels. During autumn, the colors are superb and in winter its hills are thrilling runs as part of the Scenic Drive Ski Trail. In the summer, however, the lack of outstanding views and shoreline, in a park filled with them, leads most hikers to other trails.

That makes Shauger Hill Trail the ultimate escape from crowds. Even when the viewing decks are packed and Pierce Stocking Scenic Drive is lined with crawling vehicles, you encounter few, if any, people on this foot path.

And no mountain bikers as their activity is banned from most of the national lakeshore trails.

Access and Information

From Empire, head north on M-22 and then veer to the left on M-109. Within 1.5 miles, turn west (left) at the posted entrance to Pierce Stocking Scenic Drive. The trailhead is located in the parking lot reached just before the contact station at the beginning of Pierce Stocking Scenic Drive. For additional information, stop at the Philip A. Hart Visitor Center NPS headquarters (231-326-5134; *www.nps.gov/slbe*), the nautical-looking building at the corner of M-72 and M-22 in Empire.

Hikers return to the trailhead of the Shauger Hill Trail.

On The Trail

At the east end of the large parking area there is a display sign, map box and vault toilet. From the trailhead, you quickly cross Scenic Drive and Shauger Hill Road and begin a steady uphill climb. At one point you tread between two wooded dunes before topping off in a half mile.

The trail descends before a brief climb at **Mile 1**. Within a third of a mile you cross Shauger Hill Road again and at **Mile 1.5** reach a junction map that is signposted for the Scenic Drive Ski Trail. Taking that route west leads to Pierce Stocking Scenic Drive near North Bar Overlook.

Head east (right) and the trail makes a sharp descent followed by an equally sharp ascent that may befuddle a few skiers in winter. The trail then begins a long gentle descent that lasts for a third of a mile or until you hear traffic on Pierce Stocking Scenic Drive. From the junction with the ski trail to the paved road it's a half mile and by far the most interesting stretch of the loop due to the change in the topography.

Once across Scenic Drive, the parking lot is just 200 yards away.

18

Windy Moraine Trail

🚶 🚲 ❄
Windy Moraine Trail
Distance: 1.5 miles
Hiking Time: 1 hour
Difficulty: Easy
Highlights: Beech-maple forest, Scenic vista
Map Source: Windy Moraine Trail from MichiganTrailMaps.com or Sleeping Bear Dunes National Lakeshore at www.nps.gov/slbe
Trailhead: **GPS** N44° 51' 16.27" W86° 2' 7.0"

In a park where so many trails lead across intriguing terrain to panoramic views, hiking the Windy Moraine Trail in Sleeping Bear Dunes National Lakeshore may seem anticlimactic. Maybe even boring to some. But in early October, with children in toe, this foot path is a delightful walk that leads to an interesting lesson in natural history.

The 1.5-mile loop located opposite of Pierce Stocking Scenic Drive, basically climbs its namesake moraine, a nearly 300-foot high ridge, before descending back to the trailhead. Along the way are nine numbered posts that correspond to an interpretive brochure stocked at a trailhead map box (or downloaded from *www.MichiganTrailMaps.com*). The brochure points out everything from the "edge effect" found between forests and fields and woodpecker holes to an old maple in an effort to teach the importance of diversity in nature.

Good lessons for children or their parents.

Access and Information

From the Philip Hart Visitor Center in Empire, head north on M-22 and continue north on M-109. Within 3.5 miles, just after passing the entrance to Pierce Stocking Scenic Drive, turn right on Welch Road to the trailhead and posted parking lot.

Windy Moraine Trail is open year-round and in the winter makes for a wild downhill run on Nordic skis. Visitors are required to have a weekly vehicle entrance permit, an annual park pass or a per-person pass if on foot, bicycle or motorcycle. Passes can be purchased at a self-registrar pay station at the trailhead or at the Philip Hart Visitor Center (231-326-5134; *www.nps. gov/slbe*) in Empire.

On The Trail

At the trailhead, there is parking, an information display and a vault toilet but no source of drinking water. The trail begins in a field as a mowed lane and runs parallel to M-109 before heading east to climb the moraine

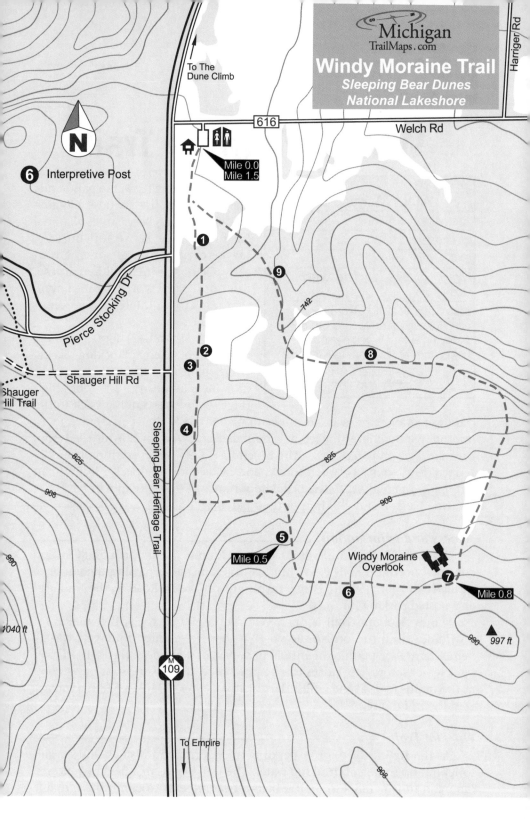

Michigan
TrailMaps.com
Windy Moraine Trail
*Sleeping Bear Dunes
National Lakeshore*

Harriger Rd

To The
Dune Climb

616

Welch Rd

Mile 0.0
Mile 1.5

N

6 Interpretive Post

❶

❾

742

Pierce Stocking Dr

❷

❸

Shauger Hill Rd

❽

Shauger
Hill Trail

825

❹

Sleeping Bear Heritage Trail

908

825

825

908

❺

Mile 0.5

908

Windy Moraine
Overlook

❼

Mile 0.8

990

❻

M 109

990

997 ft

908

To Empire

The Windy Moraine Trail during the height of fall colors.

left when the last glaciers melted 10,000 years ago. Today, part of the hill is a beech-maple forest and at **Mile 0.5** you arrive at post No. 5 and the ancient maple tree. At one time this giant was an astounding sight, a blaze of fiery reds and oranges that rivaled any lakeshore view, the reason a bench was placed beneath it. But the ancient maple was already 200 years old when age and a strong wind caught up with it.

Still the other hardwoods around it makes the red pine plantation that follows look sterile and lifeless.

In less than a mile from the trailhead, you reach post No. 7, the Windy Moraine overlook. Foliage obscures much of the view in summer, but it changes from season to season and in October it's at its best. Some leaves have fallen and what remains paints the foreground of this scenic panorama that includes Little Glen Lake.

The rest of the hike is a quick descent down the moraine through an open hillside, whose sandy soil and afternoon sun in July and August provide for an outstanding berry patch nearby. Eventually, you re-enter the old farm field and return to the trailhead at **Mile 1.5**.

Hikers begin the Dunes Trail for Lake Michigan following the Dune Climb.

19

The Dunes Trail

The Dunes Trail	
🕰 🚰 🛖 ⛰ 🐾	
Distance: 4 miles round-trip	
Hiking Time: 3 to 4 hours	
Difficulty: Challenging	
Highlights: Dune Climb, Lake Michigan beach, Shipwreck	
Map Source: The Dunes Trail from MichiganTrailMaps.com or Sleeping Bear Dunes National Lakeshore at www.nps.gov/slbe	
Trailhead: **GPS** N44° 52' 53.38" W86° 2' 26.84"	

You never know what lies at the end of a trail you've never been on. But with the Dunes Trail, arguably the most popular hike in Sleeping Bear Dunes National Lakeshore, there is no question how it begins. When hikers pull into the trailhead parking lot they immediately see a steep sandy slope rising 130 feet above them — the park's famous Dune Climb.

The start of the Dunes Trail attracts more than 300,000 people annually, with the vast majority making the climb during the summer. They struggle up the steep slope of open sand only to turn around and gleefully romp down it. After reaching the top of the slope, though, many continue on toward the Lake Michigan shoreline, a round-trip of 4 miles along a route marked by blue-tipped posts. What they expect to find at the end of the trail is a beautiful and remote stretch of beach.

What many have unexpectedly encountered since 2014 is a shipwreck. A large one.

Foul weather on Lake Michigan constantly washes up shipwreck fragments but a powerful storm in November of 2014 pushed ashore the largest piece of a wreck ever seen in the national lakeshore. Located just 300 yards from the west end of the Dunes Trail, the wreck has made one of most scenic and unique hikes in Michigan even more captivating.

The Dunes Trail is not an easy hike. Trudging through soft sand up steep dunes in the hot sun is not the same as a stroll on a beach. The route crosses the Sleeping Bear Plateau, a 4-square-mile field of perched dunes that extends to Lake Michigan to the west and Sleeping Bear Point to the north. Left behind by glaciers 11,000 years ago, the morainal plateau is composed mostly of pebbles, cobbles and even rocks.

The perched dunes actually represent only a thin veneer blanketing the glacial rubble beneath. The beautiful, rolling ridges vary from open sand or patches of beach grass and wildflowers to a lone cottonwood here and there.

It's important to remember that there is no water along the route and that the average hiker needs 30 to 40 minutes to cover a mile along the dunes. Fill a water bottle at the parking lot and pack sunglasses, a hat, and

Lake Michigan

James McBride
1857

⚠ Steep Bluffs

742

660

Mile 2.0

825

908

Michigan
TrailMaps.com

The Dunes Trail
Sleeping Bear Dunes
National Lakeshore

940

N

908

View of South
Manitou Island

742

660

Mile 1.2

742

Cottonwood
Trail

Dunes Trail

Devil's Hole

Bench

825

742

825

Trail Sign

660

Sleeping Bear
Heritge Trail

660

Dune Climb

Duneside Accessible Trail

Group
Campground

Mile 0.0

660

742

To
Empire

Glen
Lake

M 109

To
Glen Arbor

The Dunes Trail climbs several steep dunes before reaching Lake Michigan.

sunscreen. Hiking boots or tennis shoes are necessary, as attempting this trail in bare feet is not recommended. By packing a bathing suit and a beach towel you can turn this hike into a full-day affair.

Access and Information

At the corner of M-72 and M-22 in Empire, or 22 miles west of Traverse City, is the Philip Hart Visitor Center (231-326-5134; *www.nps.gov/slbe*), a nautical-looking building. From the visitor center, head north on M-22, veer left onto M-109, and in about 6 miles is the Dune Climb. A park entry permit can be purchased either at a contact station in the Dune Climb parking lot or from the visitor center.

On The Trail

At the base of the Dune Climb is a picnic area with a source of drinking water, a store, and restrooms. The trail begins with a knee-bending climb up the 45-degree slope of the dune that is slowly migrating east towards the parking area. At the top, catch your breath and enjoy the spectacular view to the east of Glen Lake and the rolling farmland that surrounds it.

To the west, in the sandy bowl at the top, is a *DUNES TRAIL* sign that clearly points the way to the first blue-tipped marker. Soon you're faced with a second dune but it's not nearly as steep as the Dune Climb. At the top, you get your first view of the Great Lake. From this high point, you descend quickly, only to climb another dune that provides a much better view of what lies ahead: a rolling terrain of dunes covered with sparse beach grass. For the next mile, you follow the posts, climbing up and down hills of sand. The trail is little more than a path of soft sand — this is where most barefoot and shirtless hikers give up and turn around.

At **Mile 1.2** you scale a dune and are greeted with the best view of South Manitou Island, on Lake Michigan's horizon. You can even see the island's historic 100-foot-high lighthouse, built in 1871 to mark the entrance of Manitou Passage. At this point, the trail descends, makes one more short

A Trail of Shipwrecks

In 2013, a November gale left behind a gift for hikers on the beach of Lake Michigan; the largest shipwreck ever to wash shore in Sleeping Bear Dunes National Lakeshore. Measuring 14 feet wide, 43 feet long and including ironwork, the wreck came to rest 300 yards south of The Dunes Trail, one of the most popular hikes in the national park.

Historians believe it is part of the *James McBride*, a 121-foot brig that was built in 1848 and launched on April Fool's Day. The two square-rigged mast vessel made history that year when she sailed to Turk Island in the Atlantic Ocean to pick up a cargo of salt and on her return stopped at Nova Scotia and added codfish to her manifest. When she arrived in Chicago on December 4, 1848 her cargo was announced as the first to be carried directly from the Atlantic to a Lake Michigan port.

In the fall of 1857, the *James McBride* sailed to the Manitou Islands, where she was loaded with a cargo of wood. On Oct. 19 she began her return trip to Chicago when the wooden vessel encountered a gale and was driven ashore. Lying in 5 to 15 feet of water just west of the tip of Sleeping Bear Point, pieces of the James McBride has been washing ashore for years. But none of them were as impressive as what appeared in November, 2013. The following spring an even larger section of the brig washed ashore 300 yards north of The Dunes Trail.

Amazing! Or is it?

One of the most intriguing aspects of Sleeping Bear Point is the many shipwrecks of the Manitou Passage. During the heyday of Great Lakes shipping from the 1860s to 1920s hundreds of vessels passed through this narrow, shoal-lined channel between the Manitou Islands and Sleeping Bear Point. And more than 50 sank, the vast majority within 400 yards of the shore, resulting in something of a shipwreck trail within the park.

Hike along the shoreline and you may find shipwrecked pieces washed ashore, particularly after storms. Begin with a visit to Sleeping Bear Point Maritime Museum, a half mile west of Glen Haven on M-209. Built in 1901, the former U.S. Lifesaving Station and boathouse have been restored and are filled with maritime exhibits. A highlight of the museum is the re-climb, and then crosses a somewhat level area for a half mile. Throughout much of June, this area is colored with wildflowers ranging from the bright yellows of hoary puccoon to the distinct oranges of wood lilies.

Reached at **Mile 2**, you don't see the beach until you're almost in the surf. Suddenly, you reach a low bluff, looking straight down at the water and the wide band of sand making up the beach.

Most people flop down on the beach right at the end of the trail. Too bad. By walking 300 yards south you reach the park's newest shipwreck that park historians believe it is part of the *James McBride* (see *A Trail of Shipwrecks*).

To return to the Dune Climb Trailhead parking lot, backtrack to the last blue-tipped post you passed and retrace your steps. Somehow the dunes are a lot steeper heading back.

enactments of 19th century rescue techniques using a beach cart and small cannon to send a line to an imaginary sinking ship. The museum is open daily from Memorial Day to Labor Day from 11 a.m. to 5 p.m., from noon to 4 p.m. daily in September and on the weekends in October.

To search for shipwrecks, pick up the brochure *Beachcombing For Shipwrecks* at the museum or the Philip Hart Visitor Center in Empire — it provides information on what to look for and how to age pieces you find. Then hit the beach and hike west toward the point. Occasionally during periods of low lake levels you can even spot large pieces of the wrecks half-buried in the sand just below the surface of the lake. The trek from Sleeping Bear Point Maritime Museum to the Dune Climb day-use area via The Dunes Trail is a one-way hike of 5 miles.

The James McBride shipwreck (photo by Friends of Sleeping Bear Dunes).

Standing in a ghost forest along the Sleeping Bear Point Trail.

20

Sleeping Bear Point Trail

Sleeping Bear Point Trail
Distance: 2.8 miles
Hiking Time: 3 hours
Difficulty: Challenging
Highlights: Ghost forests, Lake Michigan beach, Scenic vistas
Map Source: Sleeping Bear Point Trail from MichiganTrailMaps.com or Sleeping Bear Dunes National Lakeshore at www.nps.gov/slbe
Trailhead: GPS N44° 54' 33.33" W86° 2' 20.12"

Often overlooked by visitors who congregate at the Dune Climb or bike nearby Sleeping Bear Heritage Trail is the northern half of the Sleeping Bear Plateau that ends at Sleeping Bear Point. And that's amazing.

This is one of the most intriguing corners of the Sleeping Bear Dunes National Lakeshore, a place with ghost forests, windswept dunes and panoramic views of Lake Michigan. Providing access to the area is Sleeping Bear Point Trail, a 2.8-mile loop that skirts the bluffs above the point. Step-for-step, few trails in Michigan, or maybe anywhere in the Midwest, are as interesting as this route where the open dunes create excellent vantage points and the Manitou Passage — the historic shipping lane between the Manitou Islands and the mainland — provides a good reason to stop and gaze.

The trail traverses the northern half of Sleeping Bear Plateau, a 4 square-mile highland layered with perched dunes. The dunes are not as high here as they are in the southern half of the plateau but the sand is often deeper. That's because the prevailing winds from the southwest push the sand toward the Point and Sleeping Bear Bay, eroding the tops of dunes and filling in low-lying areas.

The Point is also more barren or desert-like because it's surrounded on three sides by Lake Michigan. Active dunes exist within only 1.2 miles inland of the Great Lake. Further inland, the wind loses much of its power, often allowing plants to become established on the dunes. The result here is more open sand and a more dramatic landscape of blowouts, bowls and slopes that are so gracefully curved you don't want to mar them with footprints.

Two of the more interesting features here are ghost forests — trees that have been killed but left standing by migrating sand — and Devil's Hole. Within a mile of the trailhead Sleeping Bear Point Trail passes through the middle of a ghost forest of more than two dozen trees. Devil's Hole, which can be viewed more than halfway along the trail, is a natural hole of stunted trees encircled by migrating dunes.

Lake Michigan

Sleeping Bear Point

Michigan
TrailMaps.com

Sleeping Bear Point Trail
Sleeping Bear Dunes National Lakeshore

690 ft

660

Beach Trail
0.3 mi

860

Open Dunes

Mile 0.0

Mile 2.8

M 209

To M-109

Mile 1.0

Ghost Forests

660

660

N

Mile 2.0   719 ft

742

779 ft   742

742

Devil's Hole

660

Dune Rd

660

742

The view of the Manitou Islands from the Sleeping Bear Point Trail.

Don't underestimate this short hike. Walking in sand can be strenuous and in the middle of the summer sunglasses, a wide-brimmed hat, suntan lotion and a quart of water are needed to survive the desert-like heat that radiates off the dunes. But this trek is not nearly as long or strenuous as the Dunes Trail that begins with the Dune Climb (see page 91).

Access and Information

An annual or weekly vehicle permit is required to enter the national lakeshore and can be purchased from the Philip Hart Visitor Center (231-326-5134; *www.nps.gov/slbe*) at the corner of M-22 and M-72 in Empire or at the trailhead. From the headquarters in Empire, head north on M-22 and veer off onto M-109. When M-109 turns east toward Glen Arbor, continue north on M-209 (Glen Haven Road), follow it toward Glen Haven and then west to the end. The trailhead parking area is just beyond the park's maritime museum.

There are restrooms, drinking water and some picnic tables at the maritime museum. Even when the museum is not open you can park and access the beach, a beautiful spot to spend an afternoon watching freighters cruising through the Manitou Passage.

A view of Sleeping Bear Bay from Sleeping Bear Point Trail.

On The Trail

Although occasionally referred to as the Dunes Trail-Sleeping Bear Point, this 2.8-mile loop is a separate path from the Dunes Trail that begins at the Dune Climb (see page 91). Like the Dunes Trail, this route is easy to follow — despite the shifting sand — thanks to a series of tall, blue-tipped posts that keep you on course.

The Point trail begins in the woods but quickly climbs out of the trees near a posted junction. The spur to the right leads a quarter mile through a blowout carved by the wind to a stunning beach along Lake Michigan. The loop heads left. Just beyond **Mile 0.5** you top off at the first panorama of the hike; there are views in every direction. To the west are the Manitou Islands, to the northeast the towering bluffs of Pyramid Point, to the south rolling dunes. At your feet the many shades of Lake Michigan.

The trail skirts the dune above the point and the panoramic views get even better. Eventually you swing south, descend to a plain of windswept sand and follow blue-tipped poles while crossing it. At the end of **Mile 1** you pass a ghost forest where trees were killed by the migrating dunes and then bleached white by the sun. Another ghost forest is passed and then the trail takes you on a long uphill march, topping off on a series of grass-covered dunes with views of this barren corner of the park. To the south you can peer into Devil's Hole, a rugged ravine forested at the bottom by stunted trees.

Just before **Mile 2** the trail begins to loop back and heads in a northerly direction along the crest of another high dune, where the views of Glen Lake to the east are good and any wind off Lake Michigan is refreshing. In less than a half mile, you drop into a protected spruce and birch forest. If hiking in the middle of summer, there is a sense of relief as the cooling shade of the trees is a welcome change to the hot sand. At **Mile 2.8** the trail emerges from the forest at the trailhead and parking area.

21

Alligator Hill Trail

Alligator Hill Trail
Distance: 4.3 miles
Hiking Time: 2 to 3 hours
Difficulty: Moderate
Highlights: Hardwood forested ridges, Lake Michigan vista
Map Source: Alligator Hill Trail from MichiganTrailMaps.com or Sleeping Bear Dunes National Lakeshore at www.nps.gov/slbe
Trailhead: **GPS** N44° 53' 25.58" W86° 1' 15.72"

Alligator Hill has gone full circle, and for that skiers and hikers can rejoice.

In the 1920s, the distinctive moraine pushing into the center of Glen Lake was destined for development as Day Forest Estates. David Henry Day, the lumber baron responsible for the nearby company town of Glen Haven, began to lay out an elaborate resort on the hill that included an 18-hole golf course on its north side. But the business venture didn't survive the Great Depression.

Today, Alligator Hill is protected as part of Sleeping Bear Dunes National Lakeshore with the old roads, driveways and fairways of the resort forming the backbone of its 8.3-mile trail system.

Alligator Hill is best known as a destination for Nordic skiers. Its trails form three loops that range from easy to advanced and feature plenty of long downhill runs and equally long climbs. But during the rest of the year Alligator Hill is also a good choice for anybody looking for a walk that includes the kind of Lake Michigan panorama this park is famous for.

The moraine picks up its name from a long ridge and bluff at its southeast corner that resembles the silhouette of an alligator's snout, best seen from the top of the Dune Climb to the west. Alligator Hill is the result of glacial activity when two lobes of ice that gouged out Big Glen Lake and Little Glen Lake dumped loads of sand and rock between them. An ancient Lake Michigan, which was much higher than today's lake, gradually eroded the bluffs and cut terraces and notches on the flank of the hill, including the alligator's snout. Other than to increase the mileage, the Advanced Loop and Intermediate Loop hold little interest to most hikers. Thus, the walk described here is the Easy Loop, along with the spur to Big Glen Lookout, for a 4.3-mile hike. Although the trek is rated moderate, it's a steady uphill climb in the first half.

Along with Nordic skiers and day hikers, the wide, well-marked paths are also used by equestrians as this is the only area of the national lakeshore park where horses are allowed. Mountain bikers, however, are banned from Alligator Hill.

Michigan
TrailMaps.com

Alligator Hill Trail
Sleeping Bear Dunes
National Lakeshore

Lake Michigan

Glen Arbor

D.H. Day Campground

M 109

Sleeping Bear Heritage Trail

N

South Forest Haven Dr

706 ft

Stocking Rd

Kilns

868 ft

Islands Lookout

Mile 1.4

2

990

3

Mile 3.2

1

0.2 mi

Day Farm Rd

Mile 0.0
Mile 4.3

Easy Loop

908

973 ft

1,006

908

825

742

5

Mile 3.9

0.3 mi

927 ft

4

1,000 ft

Mile 2.2

Big Glen Lookout

828 ft

908

825

908

Intermediate Loop

1.9 mi

742

660

908

908

993 ft

Little Glen Lake

Advanced Loop

Day Forest Rd

908

990

M 22

2.3 mi

815 ft

Big Glen Lake

Hikers enjoy the view from the bench at Islands Lookout.

Access and Information

From M-109, just east of the entrance to D.H. Day Campground, head south on Stocking Road. The trailhead is reached in 0.75 mile. An annual or weekly vehicle permit is required to enter the national lakeshore and can be purchased from the Philip Hart Visitor Center (231-326-5134; *www.nps.gov/slbe*) at the corner of M-22 and M-72 in Empire or at the trailhead.

On The Trail

The clearing that surrounds the main trailhead was the Day Forest Golf Club's fifth hole while the nearby row of concrete kilns was constructed in the 1950s by lumberman Pierce Stocking before he built his famous road on the west side of the park. Stocking purchased the land from David Henry Day in 1948 and used the kilns to turn scrap wood into charcoal that he bagged and sold to picnickers and campers throughout Michigan.

Post No. 1 is quickly reached and you head north (left) to reach post No. 2. You pass through one of the old fairways, though it's hard to distinguish, then in a third of a mile swing east and begin a steady climb along a wide trail that is a former road bed. It's a gentle half-mile ascent through the beech-maple forest that was heavily affected by the August, 2015 wind storm, the reason for all the down trees. The trail swings away from the edge of the ridge and at **Mile 1.4** you arrive at the posted Islands Overlook, a short walk from the main trail.

A bench is located at the edge of the bluff where you can plop down to take in the spectacular view. Below you a forest stretches north to the sandy Lake Michigan shoreline while floating on a watery horizon are North and South Manitou islands and Beaver Island. On a clear day you might even see South Fox Island and at any time a freighter might pass through the Manitou Passage. In the fall, this magnificent panorama is framed in by the shades of autumn.

Nearby, Post No. 2 clearly points out the spur to Big Glen Lookout. This segment may be a relief for some hikers as it is a wide and level path along the crest of a ridge. At the end, the spur narrows and is marked by blue blazes just before you arrive at the overlook and another bench. This view is not nearly as spectacular as Islands Lookout as you see only a small portion of Big Glen Lake and the ridges that enclose it to the east.

After backtracking to post No. 2, reached at **Mile 3**, head west (left), gently descending to post No. 3 reached within a quarter mile. Walk toward post No. 5 as the descent becomes more mellow and within a third of a mile levels out. Post No. 5 is reached at **Mile 3.9** and the last segment resumes its gentle descent through the beech-maple forest almost all the way back to the parking lot.

A Forest of Fallen Trees

On Aug. 2, 2015, three lines of storms raked across Leelanau County with winds of up to 100 mph. Hardest hit was Glen Arbor and portions of Sleeping Bear Dunes National Lakeshore that surround the village. Thousands of fallen trees toppled power lines, closed roads and damaged everything from cars and boats to homes and businesses. At the height of the summer tourism season, all roads into Glen Arbor were impassible the first night. M-109 was cleared the following day but M-22 south of town remained barricaded for four days. Power wasn't restored for five days.

Many trails were also affected including Alligator Hill and Sleeping Bear Heritage Trail. With the help of the Friends of Sleeping Bear Dunes and its army of volunteers, the Heritage Trail was reopened in 10 days.

But the nature of Alligator Hill, a high forested ridge that faced the burnt

of the storm, made clearing its trails much more challenging. The task was so daunting the goal of the park that year was to simply reopen the Easy Loop, including the popular Islands Lookout, by ski season. Using heavy equipment, trucks and chainsaws, maintenance workers began in November and in the first week alone cleared more than 2,000 trees.

Even when the entire trail is reopened, hikers, skiers and equestrians will see fallen trees everywhere. The devastation along the trail will be an unavoidable testament of the power of nature. But it will also serve as a reminder of the resiliency of a forest, that new growth is immediate and trails shaded by a canopy of foilage will return long after the windstorm has become a "remember when" story at Art's Tavern.

Alligator Hill after the windstorm.

22

Kettles Trail

🚶 🧭 ❄️ **Kettles Trail**
Distance: 3.6 miles
Hiking Time: 2 to 3 hours
Difficulty: Moderate to challenging
Highlights: Kettles, Steep forested ridges, Kettle bog
Map Source: Kettles Trail from MichiganTrailMaps.com
Trailhead: 🛰️ N44° 49' 18.18" W85° 55' 12.47"

There is a spot along the Kettles Trail where from the narrow crest of a ridge you can look into the sharp conical depression of a kettle left behind by glaciers thousands of years ago. On the other side of the ridge the slope is so steep you can't see the bottom. And in November or later, the grayish silhouettes of even higher ridges rise all around you.

It looks like a slice of the western Upper Peninsula, but it's not. The trail is in the heart of the Leelanau Peninsula, in the Bow Lakes area of Sleeping Bear Dunes Natural Lakeshore, a park known for sand dunes and beaches.

Who would have guessed that in this region of vineyards, farm stands and quaint little towns, there is a place so rugged and so remote. And so full of kettles.

A kettle is fluvioglacial landform, the result of blocks of ice splitting off from the front of a receding glacier and then buried by glacial outwash. When the ice melts a sharp-sided hole appears. An area with numerous kettles results in a rugged topography, a jumbled array of ridges, mounds and potholes.

There are at least a dozen kettles in the area that the Kettles Trail traverses, a 500-acre tract 5 miles southeast of Glen Lake. Other than three isolated kettles on North Manitou Island, this is the only place in Sleeping Bear Dunes National Lakeshore where kettles, pothole lakes and kettle bogs exist.

The geographical oddities are so rare that the park's boundary was revised in 1982 to include the Bow Lakes area, even though only the southern half is currently federal land. In 2009, a small parking lot, hiking trail and interpretive information was included in the park's General Management Plan, which should be completed soon after the release of this book.

A trailhead at the corner of Baatz and Fritz Roads provides access to 2.4 miles of signposted trail. Because some backtracking is required, Kettles Trail is a hike of 3.6 miles, with the southern portion moderate in difficulty and the northern half more challenging. Most of the system was laid out along old two-tracks, making this trail an excellent destination in the winter for

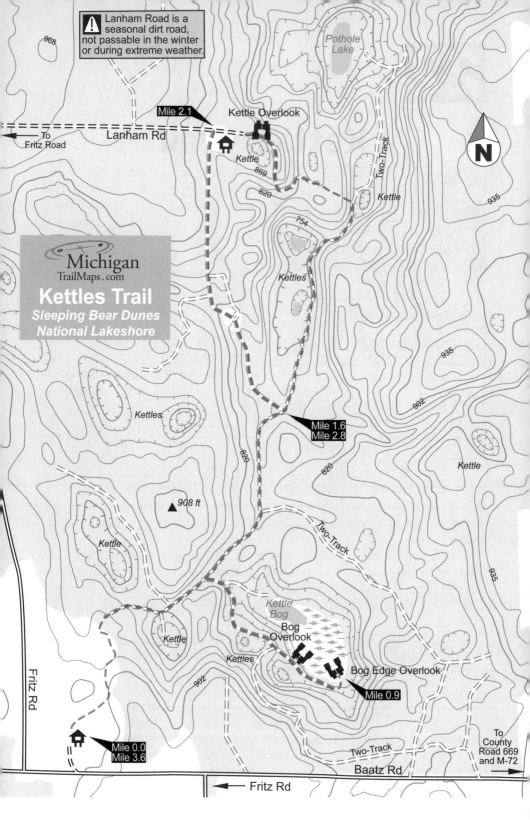

Lanham Road is a seasonal dirt road, not passable in the winter or during extreme weather.

968

Pothole Lake

Mile 2.1   Kettle Overlook

To Fritz Road   Lanham Rd

Kettle
869
820

Two-Track

Kettle

935

754

Kettles

Michigan
TrailMaps.com

Kettles Trail
Sleeping Bear Dunes
National Lakeshore

935

Kettles

902

820
820

Mile 1.6
Mile 2.8

Kettle

908 ft

Two-Track

Kettle

935

Kettle

Kettle
Bog

Kettles

Bog Overlook

Bog Edge Overlook

Mile 0.9

Fritz Rd

902

Kettle

Kettles

Mile 0.0
Mile 3.6

Two-Track

To County Road 669 and M-72

Baatz Rd

Fritz Rd

snowshoers or backcountry skiers.

Just watch out for those kettles.

Access and Information

From M-22 on the south side of Glen Lake, follow MacFarlane Road east around the lake and continue east on County Road 675. Within 4 miles of M-22, in the hamlet of Burdickville, turn south on Bow Road. After a mile, Bow Road swings east and arrives at Fritz Road. Head south for 1.4 miles to the intersection of Fritz Road and Baatz Road. The trailhead is just east on Baatz Road.

From M-72, head north on County Road 669 and in 2 miles turn west on Baatz Road. The trailhead is reached in 2.2 miles on the north side of the road.

For an update on the trail, stop by or contact the Philip Hart Visitor Center (231-326-5134; *www.nps.gov/slbe*). An annual or weekly vehicle permit is required to park at the Baatz Road trailhead.

On The Trail

The park's General Management Plan calls for part of the Kettles Trail, a segment at the beginning, to be a universally accessible path with a hard-packed surface. Future plans also call for a series of interpretive displays at the kettle bog and at the Kettle Overlook on the north end.

From the trailhead, the trail winds across an open field and within a third of a mile reaches the woods. You descend past the first kettle of the hike to arrive at the junction with the bog access spur at **Mile 0.5**. The nearly half-mile spur begins with a steady climb, topping off at a junction with an old two-track that is surrounded by kettles. There is a kettle bog to the east and two small wooded kettles to the west. You descend to the Bog Overlook and then onto the Bog Edge Overlook reached at **Mile 0.9**.

From either, there is a good view of this interesting wetland. A kettle becomes a bog when the standing water turns acidic due to decomposing organic plant matter. Kettle bogs are closed ecosystems — they have no water source other than precipitation — and serve as important ecological niches for a variety of flora and fauna species, ranging from spongy sphagnum moss and Labrador tea to bog cranberries and insect-eating sundews and pitcher plants.

Backtrack to the main Kettles Trail and head north (right). At **Mile 1.6** the loop at the north end is reached. There are climbs no matter which way you go, but following the loop in a clockwise direction (left) is an easier trek. It begins with a long climb along an old two-track to top off at 900 feet in elevation and then quickly descends to the east end of Lanham Road, reached at **Mile 2.1**. From Lanham Road, the trail continues east as another old two-track and climbs a narrow ridge to Kettle Overlook.

The overlook provides a view unlike any other in the national lakeshore. You're on the edge of a steep kettle while the north side of the ridge is even

Hikers follow one of the two-tracks that makes up much of Kettles Trail.

steeper. Ridges, some almost 1,000 feet in elevation, tower above. The trail briefly skirts the kettle and then makes a steep descent, levels off and then descends again to an old two-track on the edge of another kettle at **Mile 2.4**.

The trail follows this two-track south, steadily descending along the edge of two more kettles which may or may not have water at the bottom of them depending on how wet the year has been. After the second one, the terrain levels out and you return to the loop junction at **Mile 2.8**. From here, backtrack south to the trailhead, reached at **Mile 3.6**.

23

Bay View Trail

⚐ Bay View Trail	
Distance: 3.7 miles	
Hiking Time: 2 to 3 hours	
Difficulty: Moderate	
Highlights: Historic farms, Lake Michigan vistas	
Map Source: Bay View Trail from MichiganTrailMaps.com or Sleeping Bear Dunes National Lakeshore at www.nps.gov/slbe	
Trailhead: GPS N44° 56' 2.53" W85° 56' 55.81"	

Bay View Trail in Sleeping Bear Dunes National Lakeshore is best known as a destination for cross-country skiers, primarily because of its link to nearby Homestead Resort. The downhill ski resort rents Nordic skis and is a convenient place to warm up and re-fuel after a wintery afternoon on the trail. During the summer, the lack of impressive dune scenery that characterizes the rest of the park leads many hikers searching elsewhere for a trail to explore.

But uncrowded paths are only part of Bay View's charms. The trail system passes through a mix of beech-maple forest, old farm fields and pine plantations, while its north end features historic barns, a one-room schoolhouse and farmhouses, many of which are being restored by the National Park Service. One of three trails in the Port Oneida Rural Historic District (Pyramid Point and Sleeping Bear Heritage are the others), Bay View offers hikers historic charm as well as a stroll through meadows and woods. A fall trek often makes for a delightful afternoon of spectacular autumn colors and no people.

Who needs dunes?

The four loops of Bay View total almost 8 miles, with its premiere being a 6.4-mile hike. In 2015, the Sleeping Bear Heritage Trail (see page 123) was merged into Bay View and the southern portion of Low Trail was paved. But in the Port Oneida Rural Historic District, the Heritage Trail switches to a compacted limestone surface while the rest of Bay View's trails are foot paths with a ban on bicycles and mountain bikes. Bicycles are only allowed on the Heritage Trail.

Thus the most popular loop for hikers is the northern half of the system that includes the unpaved portion of Low Trail, Farms Trail and a side trip to Lookout Point. This 3.7-mile walk features several historic buildings and the most impressive terrain and views. The hike begins at the main trailhead on the north end of Thoreson Road, a quarter mile from M-22. The trail system can also be picked up from Olsen Farm, Miller Barn and Homestead Resort.

N

Lake Michigan

Mile 1.0

Miller Rd

Port Oneida School

Miller Barn

Mile 0.5

Lookout Point

1

2

Ridge Trail   0.5 mi

775

742

660

3

Farms Trail

Deehow Farm

Brunson Barn

Thoreson Rd

742

0.1 mi

Mile 1.9
Olsen Farm

Sunset Dr

Mile 0.0
Mile 3.7

4

Mile 2.5

Thoreson Farm

⚠ Sleeping Bear Heritage Trail switches from paved asphalt to compacted stone.

Mile 3.1

759

5

6

High Trail   0.7 mi

Bay View Trail

Low Trail Heritage Trail

0.9 mi

Michigan
TrailMaps.com

Bay View Trail
Sleeping Bear Dunes
National Lakeshore

Thoreson Rd

742

660

M-22

7

0.3 mi

Valley View Trail

Homestead Resort

825

8

0.3 mi

0.5 mi

660

908

825

990

Moosewood Trail

10

0.5 mi

9

742

660

742

0.25 mi

Homestead Rd

To Glen Arbor

Hyland Rd

The view of the Thoreson Farm from Bay View's High Trail.

Access and Information

From the town of Glen Arbor, head north on M-22 for 2 miles to reach the main entrance of the Homestead Resort and the southern trailhead for Bay View Trail. Another 2 miles north on M-22 is Thoreson Road, where you veer to the left to reach the main trailhead in a quarter mile.

A weekly vehicle entrance permit or an annual pass is required to park at the trailhead and can be purchased at the park's Philip A. Hart Visitor Center (231-326-5134; *www.nps.gov/slbe*) in Empire or the D.H. Day Campground Office (231-334-4634) just west of Glen Arbor during summer.

On The Trail

Three trails converge at the Thoreson Road trailhead. By heading north you immediately cross the dirt road and begin a long, gentle climb through a hardwood forest to arrive at post No. 1, marking the junction to Lookout Point, at *Mile 0.4*.

This side trip heads east (right) and in less than 200 yards is post No. 2 on a grassy hilltop where a nearby bench marks Lookout Point, elevation 792 feet or 208 feet above Lake Michigan. The view includes beautiful vistas

A snowshoer on his way to the Lookout Point along the Bay View Trail.

of Lake Michigan, Pyramid Point, farms and North and South Manitou Islands. Retreat back to post No. 1 and continue north (right) where the trail descends into the woods before breaking out on the edge of field, with Miller Barn at one end. You briefly tread between the open field and the edge of the shoreline bluff, where you can see the Lake Michigan surf through the trees, and then swing east.

At **Mile 1**, you cross Miller Road and pass Miller Barn. The impressive structure, along with a farmhouse that burnt down in 1940, was built in the early 1890s by John Miller. Poke around in the woods near the barn to spot some abandoned farm equipment, including what is believed to be an early corn chopper. From Miller Barn, Farms Trail becomes a mowed grassy lane as it swings past the Port Oneida School, also built in the 1890s. Nearby is a picnic table, hand pump for water and a historic outhouse complete with a half moon on the door.

Farms Trail then arrives at the junction where the Sleeping Bear Heritage Trail splits off and crosses Port Oneida Road. To the south (right) the path switches to a surface of a compacted limestone and quickly arrives at Post No. 3. Reached at **Mile 1.7**. The post marks the east end of Ridge Trail, with Lookout Point a half-mile uphill climb to the west.

Farms Trail/Heritage Trail continues south in the open fields with a view of the traffic on M-22, arriving at the Olsen Farm at **Mile 1.9**. The house and barn, built in 1918, were the first in the area with indoor plumbing. A picnic table is located near the house but there is no source of drinking water. From the Olsen Farm the trail swings behind the barn and continues south.

At **Mile 2.4**, the trail crosses Thoreson Road and quickly arrives at post No. 4. The trailhead is just a short walk to the north. To the south (left) is Low Trail, which skirts a field and wooded bluff before reaching post No. 6 at **Mile 2.8**. Beyond the post Low Trail is paved as is most of Heritage Trail. But not the spur to the west (right) that climbs more than 100 feet up the bluff, topping off at post No. 5. Your uphill effort is rewarded with sweeping views of Sleeping Bear Point jutting out into Lake Michigan.

Post No. 5 marks High Trail. Head north (right) on the mowed lane and more views follow as High Trail dips and climbs along the open top of the bluff. Within a quarter mile, the Thoreson Farm can be seen to the west, framed by Sleeping Bear Point and the Manitou Islands in the background. The farmhouse was built in 1900 by John Thoreson and Ingeborg Sakariasdatte, who emigrated from Norway. The farm has been fully restored by the National Park Service, right down to its dual privies.

Just beyond the Thoreson Farm, High Trail enters the woods and begins a descent off the north end of the bluff. At **Mile 3.5**, the trail swings east, cuts across an open field and arrives at the Thoreson Road Trailhead in less than a quarter mile.

A hiker returning to the top of Pyramid Point near the Lookout.

24

Pyramid Point Trail

✿ ▲ **Pyramid Point Trail**
Distance: 2.6 miles
Hiking Time: 2 hours
Difficulty: Moderate
Highlights: Spectacular Lake Michigan views, Perched dunes
Map Source: Pyramid Point Trail from MichiganTrailMaps.com or Sleeping Bear Dunes National Lakeshore at www.nps.gov/slbe
Trailhead: **GPS** N44° 57' 43.09" W85° 55' 47.81"

Pyramid Point in Sleeping Bear Dunes National Lakeshore was formed during the Ice Age when lobes of a glacier pushed into the adjacent Sleeping Bear and Good Harbor Bays.

The melting ice deposited layers of sand to form a high headland that at one time jutted more than 2 miles out into Lake Michigan. Eventually, the continuous pounding of waves wore down the Point to its present position but the bluffs overlooking Lake Michigan remained high and steep.

When the sport of hang gliding peaked in popularity in the late 1970s, a steady stream of pilots hiked up to Pyramid Point with flyers strapped to their backs. Using the wind currents that came up the side of the steep dune, the gliders could soar for an hour or two over Lake Michigan before heading inland to land in the large meadow to the east of the Point.

If pilots were really good, they could steer their gliders to an old farm field that surrounds the trailhead, landing practically next to their cars. If not, they would end up on the beach, faced with a steep, arduous climb up the shoreline bluff.

The hang gliders are long gone as most prefer flying inland, where they are towed into the air by a vehicle. The view from the top of Pyramid Point, however, hasn't changed a bit.

At the Lookout, hikers stand 373 feet almost straight above the lapping waters of Lake Michigan. The headland is a dramatic setting because it is the closest spot on the mainland to the Manitou Islands. You not only get an eyeful of North and South Manitou Islands but also any freighter in the area as Pyramid Point forms the south side of Manitou Passage, a popular shipping lane.

But to many, the trail's most unique aspect isn't habitat or hang gliders. It is the off-the-beaten-path location of Pyramid Point. When the famous Dune Climb is crawling with people, it's still possible to lace up a pair of hiking boots and escape the summer crowds in this corner of the park.

The vast majority of people who find their way to the Pyramid Point

Pyramid Point Trail
Sleeping Bear Dunes
National Lakeshore

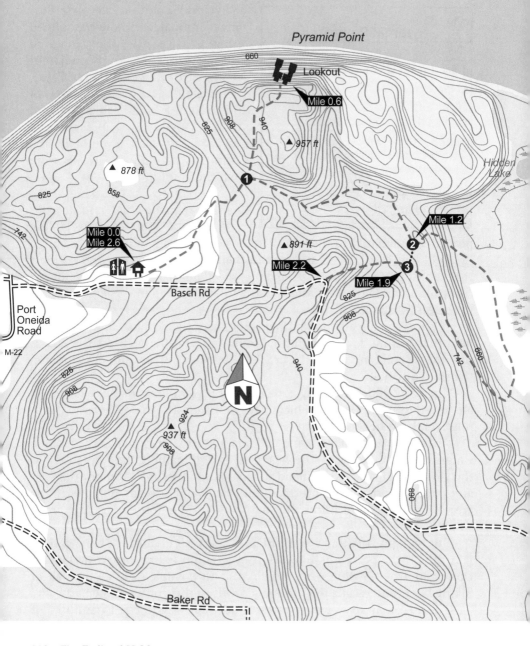

Lake Michigan

Pyramid Point

660

Lookout
Mile 0.6

▲ 957 ft

940

908

825

▲ 878 ft

858

825

1

742

Mile 1.2

2

Mile 0.0
Mile 2.6

▲ 891 ft

3

Mile 2.2

Mile 1.9

Basch Rd

825

908

Port
Oneida
Road

M-22

825

908

940

N

▲ 924 ft

937 ft

908

Hidden
Lake

742

660

890

Baker Rd

trailhead merely hike to the Lookout for the view and then return, a round trip of only 1.2 miles, with a bit of strenuous climbing near the top. Beyond the lookout, you'll usually have the rest of the trail to yourself, a 2.6-mile loop that passes through remnants of 19th century farms and century-old beech-maple forests, home to some of the largest trees in the park. In early October, the fall colors are stunning.

Access and Information

Access to the trailhead is via Basch Road, a winding dirt road that isn't plowed during the winter in an area where snowstorms sweep across Lake Michigan.

From Glen Arbor, head east then north on M-22 for 5 miles to the park's Port Oneida Historic Farm District. Within this 3,000-acre tract are more than a dozen farmhouses and barns dating back to the 1850s, many of are currently being restored by the National Park Service. When M-22 swings sharply to the east again, you continue north along Port Oneida Road for 2 miles, then east (right) on Basch Road. The dirt road climbs steadily for a third of a mile until it levels out at the trailhead parking area, where there is a vault toilet and display board but no source of drinking water.

An annual or weekly vehicle permit is required to enter the national lakeshore and can be purchased from the Philip Hart Visitor Center (231-326-5134; *www.nps.gov/slbe*) at the corner of M-22 and M-72 in Empire or at the trailhead.

On The Trail

While the outside perimeter of the Pyramid Point Trail is a 2.6-mile hike, a crossover spur, between posts No. 2 and No. 3, allows you to shorten the walk to 2 miles.

Pyramid Point Trail begins as an old two-track in a grassy meadow, the remnants of a 19th century farm. Within a quarter mile, it enters the woods and begins climbing. Eventually the ascent steepens and at **Mile 0.6** you break out of the trees at the Lookout. This 957-foot high point is a scenic spot on the edge of a perched dune, almost straight above Lake Michigan. Think twice before running down to the lake. It's a long and hard climb back up.

From the Lookout you backtrack to post No. 1, follow the fork to the left and continue the descent through a beech-maple forest. After dropping 120 feet, the trail bottoms out where a migrating dune is spilling sand among the hardwoods just before post No. 2 at **Mile 1.2**. To the west (right) is the crossover spur. Head southeast (left) and another rapid drop ends in an open area created when farmers arrived here after the Civil War. The last farm was gone by the 1930s. Today the meadow is a beautiful spot, a grassy area hemmed in by forested dunes on one side and framed by birch and beech on the other. Blue standards lead you through the length of the meadow and re-direct you back into the woods at its south end.

A family enjoys the Lake Michigan panorama at Pyramid Point.

The trail now regains all the elevation lost on the previous leg. But the 0.4-mile ascent is a scenic one if the leaves have dropped, with a view of the entire meadow and the Lake Michigan shoreline. At post No. 3, reached at **Mile 1.9**, you head west (left) for the final leg to Basch Road. This stretch includes the steepest climb of the trail, with a deep ravine running along its south side. At **Mile 2.2**, you break out at the dirt road, where a post directs you west (right). The remainder of the hike is a downhill walk along Basch Road, which winds through a forest so thick that its foliage forms a canopy. Even on the hottest days, this is cool end to a hilly hike.

25

Good Harbor Bay Trail

Good Harbor Bay Trail	
Distance: 2.8 miles	
Hiking Time: 2 to 3 hours	
Difficulty: Easy	
Highlights: Lake Michigan beach, Coastal dunes	
Map Source: Good Harbor Bay Trail from MichiganTrailMaps.com or Sleeping Bear Dunes National Lakeshore at www.nps.gov/slbe	
Trailhead: GPS	N44° 56' 12.90" W85° 51' 25.41"

Within Sleeping Bear Dunes National Lakeshore, a park of towering dunes and rolling ridges, Good Harbor Bay Trail is the rare exception. This 2.8-mile loop is almost entirely flat, a trail where a change in elevation is better measured in inches not feet.

A narrow strip of low coastal dunes surround the picnic area and extends east along the shoreline. But further inland is a mix of forest and wetlands. The area was part of an ancestral Lake Michigan until 11,000 years ago when the water level dropped. Good Harbor Bay and its beach appeared in stages and the low ridges that lie parallel to Lake Michigan inland are not dunes but ancient shorelines.

People new to Nordic skiing love this trail. Its level contour — the grade never exceeds 10 percent — and the abundance of lake-effect snow off the bay makes it easy to master the kick-and-glide technique of traditional cross-country skiing. The forests tends to hold the snow late into the season.

Birders are also fond of the Good Harbor Bay. From April through June and again in September they arrive to scope the shoreline for migrating shorebirds and Lake Michigan for waterfowl. The pines, cedars and scrub in the dune transition forest are also traditional nesting grounds for Prairie Warbler, a state-endangered species which nests on the ground.

For hikers it's a different story. For many the numerous outstanding trails elsewhere in the national lakeshore makes Good Harbor Bay and its lack of dramatic scenery a mundane choice at best. But the trailhead is located in a pleasant little picnic area that to the east looks out towards Whaleback Bluff south of Leland and North Manitou Island to the north. Right in front of it is a nearly endless beach. A family with young children could spend an afternoon here, hiking in the woods and playing in the surf and then top off the day with a picnic dinner that includes a tableside view of Lake Michigan. If they stay long enough and maybe they'll catch a sunset.

Access and Information

Good Harbor Bay is roughly halfway between Leland and Glen Arbor

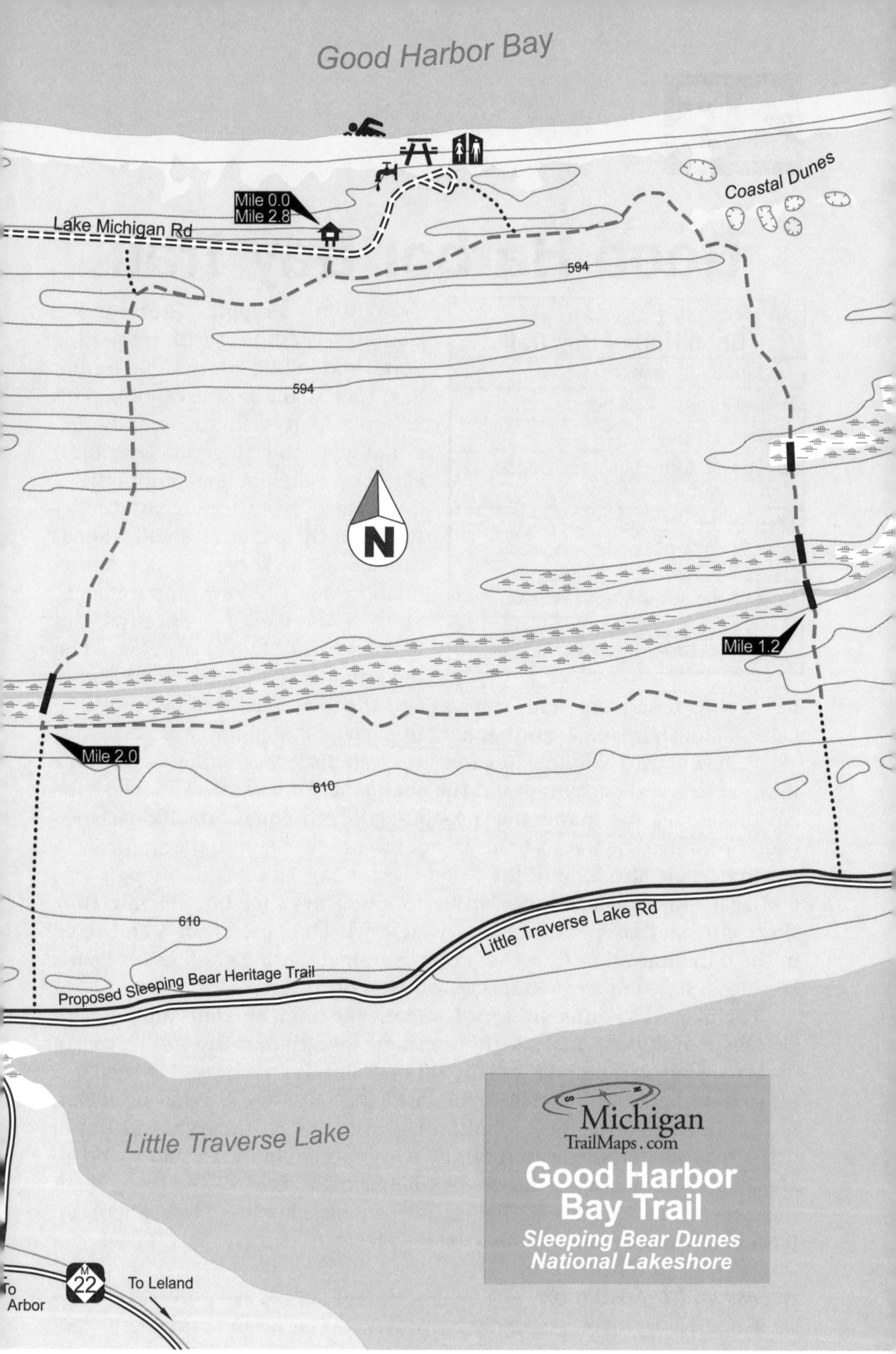

Good Harbor Bay

Coastal Dunes

Mile 0.0
Mile 2.8

Lake Michigan Rd

594

594

N

Mile 1.2

Mile 2.0

610

610

Little Traverse Lake Rd

Proposed Sleeping Bear Heritage Trail

Little Traverse Lake

Michigan
TrailMaps.com

**Good Harbor
Bay Trail**
*Sleeping Bear Dunes
National Lakeshore*

M 22

To Leland

To
Arbor

Looking for Petoskey stones on the beach at Good Harbor Bay.

along M-22, 9 miles from either one. From M-22, turn north on Bohemian Road (County Road 669) and follow it to the lakeshore where you will turn east on Lake Michigan Road to the trailhead and picnic area at the end.

The trail is open year-round and all visitors are required to have a weekly vehicle entrance permit, an annual park pass or a per-person pass if they arrive on foot, bicycle or motorcycle. Passes can be purchased from the Philip Hart Visitor Center (231-326-5134; *www.nps.gov/slbe*) in Empire.

On The Trail

From the trailhead along Lake Michigan Road, the trail enters the woods and immediately arrives at a junction. Head east to follow the loop in a clockwise direction and within a 0.3 mile you arrive in the semi-open of strip of coastal dunes. Patches of sand appear here between the shrubs and if the day is windy you can easily hear the surf crashing along the shoreline. At **Mile 0.6** the trail swings south to enter a pine-oak forest and begin crossing a series of very low rises that at one time were ancient shorelines.

Eventually the trail begins crossing foot bridges through low-lying wooded wetlands and at **Mile 1.2** uses a small foot bridge to cross an unnamed stream. On the other side you follow what appears to be an old railroad bed briefly before the trail swings west (right) at a well-marked junction where it returns to being a narrow path. The rail bed continues south but you hike west (right) through a predominately beech-maple forest that is far cry from a view of Lake Michigan but can be beautiful in October. At **Mile 2** the trail swings north and immediately follows a long stretch of planking across another stretch of wetland and then the stream itself.

The final segment remains in the forest as you close in on the shoreline. At **Mile 2.6** you pass an social path that veers to the right for Lake Michigan Road and then swing to east (right) to return to the junction and pop out at the trailhead at **Mile 2.8**.

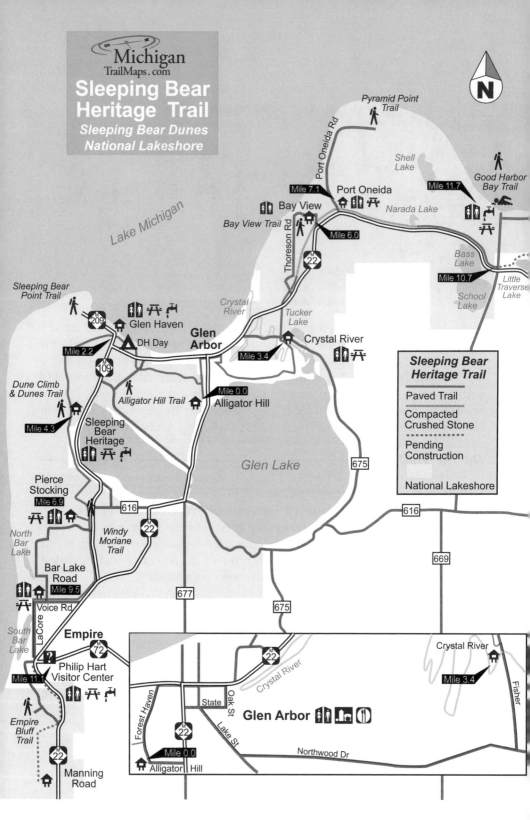

Michigan
TrailMaps.com

Sleeping Bear Heritage Trail
Sleeping Bear Dunes National Lakeshore

N

Pyramid Point Trail

Port Oneida Rd

Shell Lake

Mile 7.1

Port Oneida

Mile 11.7

Good Harbor Bay Trail

Bay View

Narada Lake

Bay View Trail

Mile 6.0

Thoreson Rd

22

Lake Michigan

Bass Lake

Mile 10.7

Little Traverse Lake

School Lake

Sleeping Bear Point Trail

209

Glen Haven

Crystal River

Tucker Lake

Glen Arbor

Crystal River

Mile 2.2

DH Day

109

Mile 3.4

Sleeping Bear Heritage Trail

Dune Climb & Dunes Trail

Alligator Hill Trail

Mile 0.0

Alligator Hill

Paved Trail

Compacted Crushed Stone

Mile 4.3

Pending Construction

Sleeping Bear Heritage

Glen Lake

National Lakeshore

675

Pierce Stocking

Mile 6.9

616

North Bar Lake

Windy Moriane Trail

616

616

22

669

Bar Lake Road

Mile 9.5

675

Voice Rd

677

675

South Bar Lake

LaCore

Empire

72

Crystal River

Philip Hart Visitor Center

22

Crystal River

Mile 11.1

Forest Haven

State

Oak St

Glen Arbor

Mile 3.4

Fisher

Empire Bluff Trail

22

Lake St

22

Mile 0.0

Northwood Dr

Manning Road

Alligator Hill

26

Sleeping Bear Heritage Trail

Sleeping Bear Heritage Trail	
Distance: 11.1 miles or 11.7 miles	
Biking Time: 3 to 4 hours for either	
Difficulty: Moderate to challenging	
Highlights: Historic Glen Haven, Lake Michigan beaches, Dune Climb	
Map Source: Sleeping Bear Heritage Trail from MichiganTrailMaps.com or Friends of Sleeping Bear Dunes at sleepingbeartrail.org	
Trailhead: **GPS**	N44° 53' 21.04" W85° 59' 33.5"

Sleeping Bear Heritage Trail is a paved path with attitude.

Most hard-surfaced trails, many of them leftover rail beds, are long, straight and level without so much as a dip or a curve. Not this trail. The Heritage Trail climbs over impressive ridges, swings past imposing sand dunes, dips around lakes, crosses streams and wetlands on long boardwalks. In between the stretches of rolling topography are historic farmsteads, a ghost town and sweeping views from the heart of Michigan's most popular national park.

In a region that already boosts some of the state's most scenic paths, Sleeping Bear Heritage Trail is destined to be the crowning jewel when it's finished.

The seed for the paved trail was planted in 2005 when the Leelanau Scenic Heritage Route Committee pitched the idea to the National Park Service. It was noted that while Sleeping Bear Dunes National Lakeshore had more than 100 miles of hiking trails and even 9 miles of equestrian trails, none were paved and suitable for recreational use by cyclists, wheelchair users, runners pushing baby strollers and rollerbladers.

After years of reports, studies and environmental assessments, a 27-mile trail through the park was on the drawing board, extending from Good Harbor Trail (County Road 651) on the northern boundary of the park southwest past Empire to Manning Road, running parallel to M-22 and M-109 for much of the way.

Most of the non-motorized trail is an asphalt-paved, 10-foot-wide path accessed by 11 trailheads and lined with amenities ranging from restrooms and picnic areas to benches along the steepest slopes. The exception is a 3.1-mile segment through the Port Oneida Rural Historic District where the trail surface is compacted crushed limestone.

The Heritage Trail has been developed in segments, a $10 million to $12 million project that requires more than a decade to complete. For the most part, the trail has been built over old logging roads, abandoned rail beds and

Nordic skiers on the Sleeping Bear Heritage Trail (Friends of Sleeping Bear Dunes photo).

existing trails to keep forest disruption to a minimum. Where the trail runs though the villages of Glen Arbor and Empire, users are diverted to low-traffic roads.

The first section, opened in 2012 to rave reviews, is a 4.3-mile segment anchored at one end by charming Glen Arbor and at the other end by the popular Dune Climb. In between, it passes views of Lake Michigan, towering sand dunes and the century-old storefronts of the restored company town of Glen Haven. This is by far the most popular stretch of the Heritage Trail. In 2014, the 6.8-mile segment from the Dune Climb to Empire was added and a year later the trail was extended 6.5 miles north to the historic farming district of Port Oneida. In 2016, another 3.6-mile segment pushed the trail east to Good Harbor Bay.

Mileposts along the Heritage Trail begin with Mile 0.0 at the Dune Climb with mile markers to the south starting with "S" (S01.0) and those heading north towards Glen Arbor starting with "N" (N01.0).

But Glen Arbor serves as the hub of the system and the first segment had no more been paved than bike rental shops and other services appeared in town. In 2014, the Bay Area Transportation Authority (BATA) set up a Bike-N-Ride bus service for the Heritage Trail similar to what is offered for the Leelanau Trail. For that reason and because of the popularity of the ride from Glen Arbor to the Dune Climb, the Heritage Trail is described here as an 11.1-mile ride from the Alligator Hill Trailhead to Empire and an 11.7-mile ride from the Alligator Hill Trailhead to Good Harbor Bay at the north end of County Road 669.

In winter, the Friends of Sleeping Bear Dunes grooms segments of the trail for both classic Nordic skiers and skaters as well as a lane for snowshoers.

Access and Information

Just south of Glen Arbor, the Heritage Trail is picked up at the Alligator Hill Trailhead, reached by turning west on Forest Haven Drive off of M-22 a half-mile south of town. The trailhead also serves the Alligator Hill Trail (see page 101). Other trailheads to the east include Crystal River near the County Road 675 and Fisher Road, Bay View on Thoreson Road just north of M-22 and Port Oneida on Port Oneida Road just north of M-22.

Trailheads between Glen Arbor and Empire include Glen Haven on M-209 (Glen Haven Road) just north of M-109, the Dune Climb day-use area on M-109, Pierce Stocking at the start of Pierce Stocking Drive off M-109, Bar Lake Road 0.7 mile west of M-22 via Voice Road, and the Sleeping Bear Dunes National Lakeshore Visitor Center near the corner of M-22 and M-72 in Empire. The facilities at the trailheads vary, with most featuring a toilet, information kiosk and parking. Those with drinking water include Glen Haven, Sleeping Bear Heritage and the Philip Hart Visitor Center.

From late May to late October, BATA offers Bike-N-Ride service on Route 11 that extends from Traverse City to Empire with stops in Glen Arbor. The specially-equipped buses can carry 11 bikes, including child trailers, and depart daily from the Hall Street Transfer Station in Traverse City from late June through Labor Day and on weekends the rest of the season. Stops along the Heritage Trail include the Homestead Resort, Glen Arbor, the Dune Climb, Pierce Stocking Drive, and Empire, so it's possible to ride a portion of the trail. In Glen Arbor, the stop is at the corner of M-22 and Oak Street.

Bikes are transported as part of a regular $3 fare that is paid on the bus in cash or with a BATA FlashFare card. It's first-come-first-serve, so in July and August it's wise to get to the stops early. For a complete list of stops and times, contact BATA (231-941-2324; *bata.net/bikenride*).

A Sleeping Bear Dunes National Lakeshore annual or weekly vehicle pass is required to use most of the trail. Visitors need to show a pass at the contact stations at the Dune Climb and Pierce Stocking Scenic Drive, or place it on their vehicle dashboard if departing from a NPS trailhead or along a road. Passes can be purchased from the Philip Hart Visitor Center, at contact stations or self-registration stations at the trailheads.

For more information, go to the Sleeping Bear Heritage Trail website (*sleepingbeartrail.org*) or the Friends of Sleeping Bear Dunes website (*friendsofsleepingbear.org*). For more information about the national lakeshore, contact or stop at the Philip Hart Visitors Center (231-326-5134; *www.nps. gov/slbe*). Located near the corner of M-72 and M-22, the center is open daily from 8 a.m. to 6 p.m. from Memorial Day to Labor Day and 8:30 a.m. to 4 p.m. the rest of the year.

On The Trail

Glen Arbor to Empire

The ride from Glen Abor to Empire is an 11.1-mile outing, with the first section to the Dune Climb by far the busiest stretch of the Heritage Trail.

Glen Arbor

Mile 0.0

Forest Haven Dr

Mile 0.3

Michigan
TrailMaps.com
Sleeping Bear Heritage Trail

Lake Michigan

1006

Islands Lookout

M 109

908

927 ft ▲

908

825

Alligator Hill Trail

828 ft ▲

742

660

Mile 1.9

D.H. Day Campground

Stocking Rd

Day Forest Rd

Glen Haven Historic Village

Mile 2.2

Day Farm Rd

M 209

Sleeping Bear Point Maritime Museum

Sleeping Bear Heritage Trail

Dune Valley Rd

742

Glen Lake

M 109

Dune Climb

Mile 4.3

Sleeping Bear Point Trail

660

Group Campground

Dunes Trail

742

660

In Glen Arbor, the trail shares the trailhead with the Alligator Hill Trail on Forest Haven Drive, 300 yards west of M-22.

Head north on Forest Haven Drive to pick up the well-posted Heritage Trail within a third of a mile and then west on the paved path into a forest that was devastated by the August 2015 storm. There will be down timber on both sides of the paved path for years to come. Though the trail skirts Alligator Hill at this point, it remains a level ride in the summer and an easy ski in the winter. The Heritage Trail crosses M-109, a busy state highway in the summer, at *Mile 1.9* and then skirts D.H. Campground, where there is access to toilets, drinking water, a beautiful beach and a picnic area.

At *Mile 2.2*, the trail enters historic Glen Haven and crosses M-209. Founded in 1857 when a sawmill was built, Glen Haven was developed as a deep-water port to service shipping traffic with firewood, lumber and other supplies. The village was at its peak in 1881 when it featured 11 buildings, including an inn, a store, blacksmith shop, wagon shop, and school. Steamship service continued to Glen Haven until the late 1920s when the Great Depression facilitated the end of its role as a port. Eventually, its massive dock deteriorated and the village was abandoned.

The most distinctive building seen from the trail is the bright red Glen Haven Canning Company . Originally built as a warehouse, it was converted to what was then a state-of-the-art cannery for cherries in the early 1920s. Today it is a seasonal maritime museum filled with historic boats that once plied the waters between Glen Haven and the Manitou Islands. Nearby is a fully restored blacksmith shop and the Glen Haven General Store. All three museums are open daily from Memorial Day weekend through Labor Day.

After crossing M-209, the trail enters a semi-open meadow and begins a long, gentle climb, topping out at the west end of Dunes Valley Road at *Mile 3* where it swings south and re-enters the woods. A gentle descent leads past the Group Campground, where toilets and drinking water are available.

Riders then pass some of the trail's most impressive terrain. On one side of the trail is a lush green forest, on the other a towering dune so steep that occasionally small avalanches of snow rumble down it. For all the change in elevation surrounding the path, this is an amazingly level and easy trail.

The Heritage Trail merges into the park's Duneside Accessible Trail, a half-mile path featuring a series of interpretive displays and benches, before arriving at the Dune Climb at *Mile 4.3*. The popular day-use area has restrooms, picnic tables, drinking water, an extensive parking area and a small seasonal store. Looming overhead is the imposing Dune Climb and the start of the Dunes Trail (see page 91).

The Heritage Trail departs the Dune Climb to the south and within a mile changes from flat to hilly. The first steep hill is encountered at *Mile 5.8* where there is a bench at the top. You descend to Greenan Road, follow it briefly to the west (right) and then continue south by climbing the longest hill of the ride, one that gains almost 100 feet in a quarter mile. Nicknamed "the Bear," it is lined with benches. You descend the backside and bottom

Heritage Trailhead at the Dune Climb (Friends of Sleeping Bear Dunes photo).

out near the spur to the Pierce Stocking Trailhead at **Mile 6.9**.

After crossing Pierce Stocking Drive, the Heritage Trail climbs again, followed by a long and pleasant downhill run. For the next 1.6 miles, cyclists enjoy a free ride that includes speeding past the M-22 and M-109 intersection. At **Mile 9**, the trail swings west and climbs one more hill before arriving at the intersection of Voice Road and Bar Lake Road, reaching the Bar Lake Road Trailhead at **Mile 9.5**. North Bar Lake, a popular day-use area and beach, is 1.4 miles to the north via Bar Lake Road. The Heritage Trail swings south at LaCore Road and ends. You follow LaCore Road south to Empire, reaching the Philip Hart Visitor Center at **Mile 11.1**.

From Empire, plans call for extending the trail 2.3 miles south along M-22 to a proposed trailhead at Manning Road and Norcronk Road on the Leelanau/Benzie Countyline. For those using the BATA Bike-N-Ride service, the bus stops in Empire at the gas station on the corner of M-22 and M-72.

Glen Arbor to Good Harbor Bay

East of Glen Arbor, the Heritage Trail follows roads through town and for 3.4 miles to the Crystal River Trailhead. From the Alligator Hill Trailhead, head north on Forest Haven Drive and then east (right) on M-109 and M-22 through the heart of downtown Glen Arbor. *Keep a watchful eye on traffic!* There is a dedicated bike lane along M-22 but in the summer this five-block stretch often bustles with cars, pedestrians and cyclists.

Turn south (right) on Oak Street to escape the maddening summer scene and then west (right) for a block on State Street. Turn south (left) on Lake Street and within a third of a mile go east (left) on Northwoods Drive, a pleasant road to pedal because of its leafy canopy and light traffic. Glen Lake is just to the south but usually hidden by homes and foliage. At **Mile 3**, turn north (left) on Fisher Road and in less than a half mile you cross over beautiful Crystal River and arrive at the Crystal River Trailhead.

From the trailhead the Heritage Trail briefly skirts County Road 675 as a dedicated path before crossing it and heading north into the wetlands west of Tucker Lake. An 800-foot boardwalk provides passage and makes for an ideal place to pause and look for wildlife. At **Mile 4.3**, the Heritage Tail crosses M-22 near the Homestead Resort, whose reception center is the first stop along the trail for the BATA Bike-N-Ride service from Traverse City.

Another hilly stretch is encountered after crossing M-22. You immediately climb a hill and then descend to Thoreson Road, where post No. 9 of Bay View Trail (see page 109) is located. You climb again and then enjoy a long downhill run. At **Mile 5.5** is post No. 6, where the surface changes from asphalt to compacted crushed limestone as the Heritage Trail enters the Port Oneida Rural Historic District.

This 3,000-acre portion of the national lakeshore protects more than 145 structures, many of them barns, sheds and farmhouses. It's the largest publicly-owned agricultural landscape in the country, preserving the architecture and technology that was common to subsistence farms of the upper Great Lakes region during the early 1900s. While dunes are the trademark of the Heritage Trail south of Glen Arbor, it is the turn-of-the-century farms that make the eastern half of the trail so intriguing, a rare collection in a setting that is, for most part, free from modern development.

At **Mile 6**, the Heritage Trail crosses Thoreson Road, which leads west to the Bay View Trailhead, and in another half mile arrives at the Charles Olsen Farm with its impressive red barn and steel and wooden silo. The classic farmhouse and barn were built in 1918 and have been restored by the park.

Continuing in a northeast direction, the Heritage Trail passes post No. 3, marking a spur of the Bay View Trail that leads a half mile up a ridge to Lookout Point. Just beyond it you arrive at Port Onieda Road at **Mile 7.1**. On the west side of the road is the Port Oneida Schoolhouse built in the 1890s and a classic outhouse. On the east side is the Kelderhouse farm that was a central gathering place for Port Oneida residents in the early 1900s. The farmhouse was built around 1910 and at one time or another was used as a grocery store, telephone exchange and post office.

The Heritage Trail swings around the Kelderhouse Cemetery to M-22 and then begins to skirt the state highway, remaining within view of it most of the time. Near the intersection with Wheeler Road at **Mile 8** you arrive at the Lawr Farm that dates to 1890. Just beyond the farm the trail crosses Basch Road and passes through a roadside rest area with two picnic tables.

Within a quarter mile, the trail swings away from M-22 and enters the woods, arriving at the west side of Narada Lake at **Mile 8.7**. Tucked into the trees nearby is the North Unity School, a one-room log structure that was built in 1860. At this point the Heritage Trail skirts the lake by dipping down to cross its marshy south end via a 1,000-foot boardwalk. On the other side you climb to the Goffer farmhouse overlooking Narada Lake on M-22.

Reached at **Mile 9**, the Goffer Farm is owned by the National Park Service but is privately leased. It represents the eastern boundary of the Port

The Very Good Friends of Sleeping Bear Dunes

Trails may be in public parks but often it is non-profit groups of volunteers that raise the funds to build them and then assist in the maintenance after the paths are open. Such is the case with the Friends of Sleeping Bear Dunes.

Founded in 1994, the group was reorganized in 2004 after Sleeping Bear Dunes National Lakeshore was hit by deep cuts in the federal budget. Today Friends of Sleeping Bear Dunes overseas an army of more than 700 volunteers who work in the park throughout the year.

Among their programs are Adopt-A-Beach and Adopt-A Trail in which volunteers hike a stretch of shoreline to pick up trash or a chosen trail to interact with visitors. The Trail Ambassador program for the Sleeping Bear Heritage Trail involves 120 "ambassadors" who spend time on the paved path while another 35 Friends are volunteer groomers who set track and skating lanes for skiers in the winter.

It is Friends who mow the fields in the Port Oneida Rural Historic District, staff the Sleeping Bear Point Maritime Museum and the Cannery Boat Museum in Glen Haven and spearhead the development of new trails, ranging from Kettles Trail in the Bow Lakes Region to the proposed Echo Valley Mountain Bike Trail, the park's first dedicated to off-road cycling.

Want to be a Friend? You can join the organization, volunteer or donate to their projects by visiting the group's website (*friendsofsleepingbear.org*).

Just a few of the good Friends of Sleeping Bear Dunes.

Oneida Rural Historic District. Beyond it, the Heritage Trail resumes being an asphalt-paved path. The trail remains close to M-22 for the next mile, passing views of Bass Lake on the south side of M-22 and then Bass Lake Cottages. A quarter mile beyond the resort Heritage Trail ends at County Road 669 (Bohemian Road), reached at *Mile 10.7*.

Plans call for extending the trail another 5.2 miles past Little Traverse Lake to the north end of County Road 651 (Good Harbor Trail). The day-use beach area, with restrooms, a picnic area and parking, would serve as the eastern trailhead for the Heritage Trail. Alternatively, Bohemian Road ends in a mile to the north at another day-use area on Good Harbor Bay, with toilets, drinking water, picnic tables and a beautiful beach.

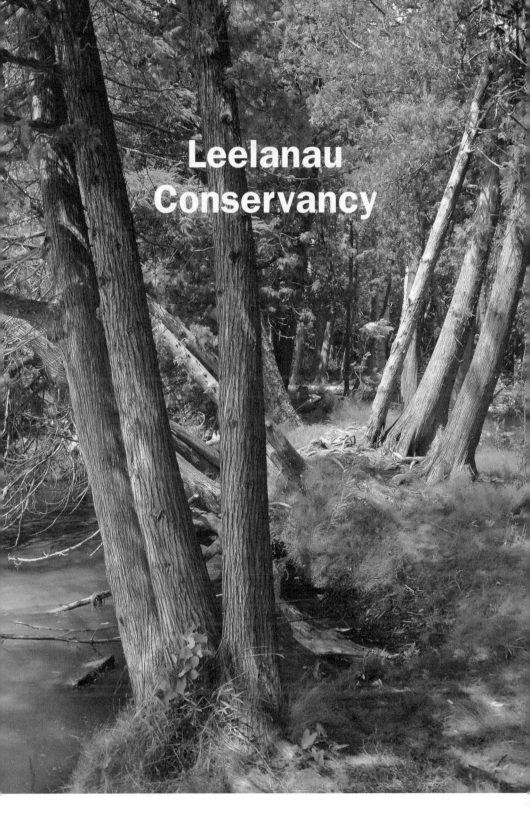

Leelanau
Conservancy

A hiker enjoying Krumwiede Forest Reserve in early fall.

27

Krumwiede
Forest Reserve

Krumwiede	
Distance: 1.7 miles	
Hiking Time: 1 hour	
Difficulty: Moderate	
Highlights: High forested ridge, Glacial erratic	
Map Source: Krumwiede Forest Reserve that can be downloaded from MichiganTrailMaps.com or Leelanau Conservancy at leelanauconservancy.org	
Trailhead: GPS	N44° 54' 16.63" W85° 54' 37.34"

There are no spectacular views from Krumwiede Forest Reserve.

There are no panoramas of Lake Michigan or islands or golden dunes towering above the shoreline. In the middle of the summer, when the foliage is thick and green, there are no views at all. But in October, climb the ridge that dominates the 110-acre tract and the hardwoods will be burning with autumn reds, yellows, oranges and purples.

At times like this every step of your hike is a sight to behold.

Located almost due east of Glen Arbor and within a mile of Sleeping Bear Dunes National Lakeshore in three different directions, Krumwiede is Leelanau Conservancy's first forest reserve. The reserve, as opposed to a preserve, is a forest that is managed to maintain, even improve, the biological diversity of the trees through periodic selective harvesting.

When the Krumwiede family donated a conservation easement on the land in 1997, they reserved the right to manage the forest as a commercial timberland. When they donated the land outright to the Leelanau Conservancy in 2007, the commercial harvests continued as a way to demonstrate and promote sustainable timber production.

Krumwiede is an excellent example of the powerful glacial activity that took place in Michigan more than 10,000 years ago. Signs of glaciers are everywhere. The 241-foot high ridge is a lateral moraine, a parallel ridge of debris deposited along the sides of a glacier. The valley west of the ridge, which Wheeler Road winds through, is an ancient glacial drainage channel. Crowning the ridge, right along the trail, is an erratic, a huge boulder that was deposited after the glaciers receded.

Winding up, over and around the Krumwiede ridge are the reserve's 2.2 miles of trails. Forestry Loop is the perimeter of the system, a 1.8-mile trek. This hike, however, is a 1.7-mile outing that includes Ridgeline Trail, which departs from the Forestry Loop to follow the crest of the ridge. While

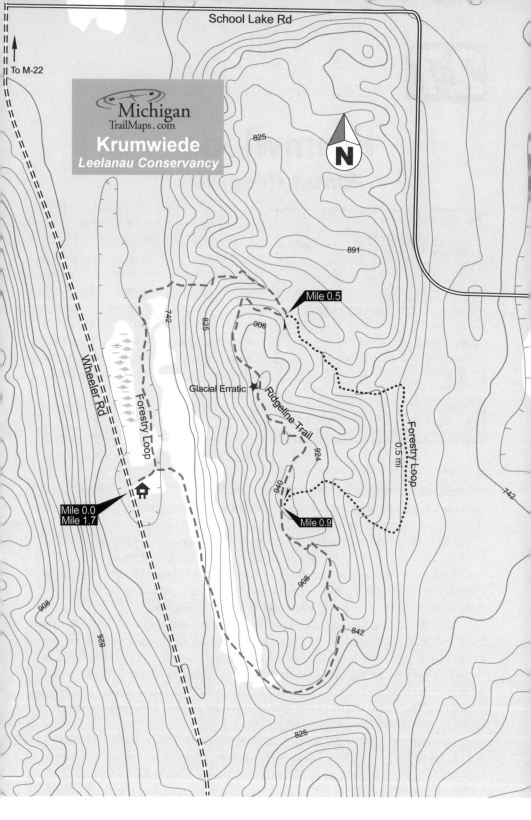

School Lake Rd

To M-22

Michigan
TrailMaps.com

Krumwiede
Leelanau Conservancy

N

825

891

Mile 0.5

825

742

908

Glacial Erratic

Ridgeline Trail

924

Forestry Loop
0.5 mi

946

Mile 0.9

Wheeler Rd

Forestry Loop

Mile 0.0
Mile 1.7

908

742

908

842

825

908

825

Wild blackberries can be found in Krumwiede Forest Reserve.

mountain bikes are banned from the reserve, Krumwiede is an excellent destination for hikers, snowshoers and backcountry Nordic skiers. Winter visitors often choose the Forestry Loop, a former two-track that now makes for a wide trail and is much more forgiving to an occasional spill.

Access and Information

From Glen Arbor, head northeast on M-22 and within 6 miles turn south (right) on Wheeler Road. The Krumwiede Forest Reserve trailhead is on the east side of the road, 2.2 miles south of M-22. For more information, contact the Leelanau Conservancy (231-256-9665; *leelanauconservancy.org*).

On The Trail

The Krumwiede Trailhead has parking for three or four vehicles but no other facilities. Just beyond the information display is the junction of the return from the Forestry Loop. Head north (left) and the trail begins in a lightly wooded strip bordering a grassy field on one side and a northern wet meadow on the other. Within a quarter mile the Forestry Loop swings east and begins climbing as an old two-track.

The trail is wide and the climb steady but not steep. At **Mile 0.5** is the first posted junction with Ridgeline Trail. Forestry Loop is the former two-track that descends to the southeast (left) before re-climbing the ridge. The descent along this half-mile stretch is sharp and the climb back to the crest of the ridge even steeper as you gain 150 feet in less than a quarter mile.

Ridgeline Trail splits off to the west (right) as a true foot path and begins with a short ascent before following the undulating crest of the forested ridge. Other than possibly in winter, there are no views through the trees. But you know you're on a ridge — and a tall one at that — as you look down steep slopes to the west. At **Mile 0.7**, the trail passes a huge glacial erratic.

Ridgeline Trail reaches its second junction with Forestry Loop at **Mile 0.9**, close to the high point of the ridge at almost 950 feet. Continue right and the trail descends steadily for almost a half mile, bottoming out where Forestry Loop swings north into an open field. Continue for almost another quarter mile to reach the trailhead. In summer, if your timing is right, wild raspberries will be ripe for the picking.

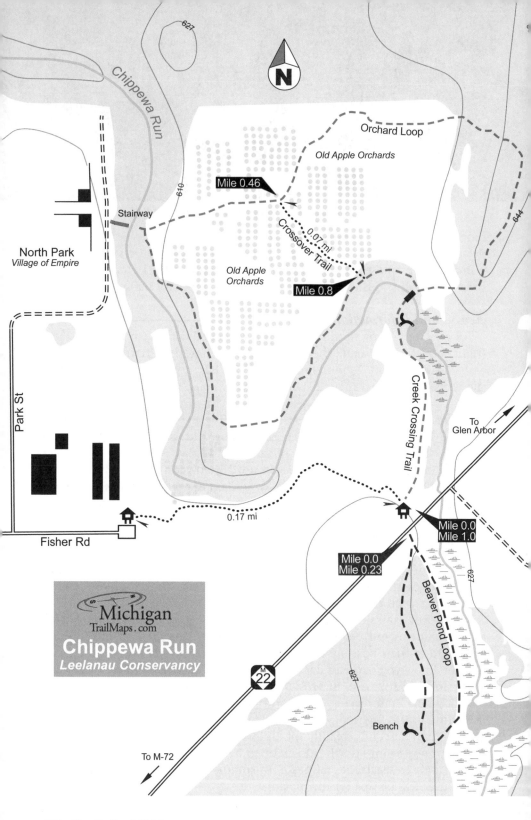

627

N

Chippewa Run

Orchard Loop

Old Apple Orchards

649

Mile 0.46

Stairway

North Park
Village of Empire

Crossover Trail

0.07 mi

Old Apple
Orchards

Mile 0.8

644

Creek Crossing Trail

To
Glen Arbor

Park St

Fisher Rd

0.17 mi

Mile 0.0
Mile 1.0

Mile 0.0
Mile 0.23

627

S
Michigan
TrailMaps.com
Chippewa Run
Leelanau Conservancy

Beaver Pond Loop

M 22

627

Bench

To M-72

Chippewa Run
Natural Area

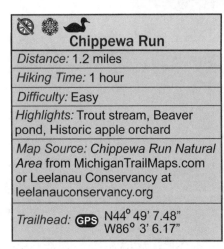

Chippewa Run
Distance: 1.2 miles
Hiking Time: 1 hour
Difficulty: Easy
Highlights: Trout stream, Beaver pond, Historic apple orchard
Map Source: Chippewa Run Natural Area from MichiganTrailMaps.com or Leelanau Conservancy at leelanauconservancy.org
Trailhead: GPS N44° 49' 7.48" W86° 3' 6.17"

Straddling M-22 on the edge of Empire, Chippewa Run Natural Area is a mere quarter mile from Sleeping Bear Dunes National Lakeshore, no doubt the reason many people zip right past it. Or don't even know it exists.

The 110-acre preserve doesn't have sand dunes or long stretches of Lake Michigan shoreline but does feature an interesting history and a variety of habitats that make for excellent birding. But for many, its most important role is how the preserve serves as a natural buffer to the continuous pressure of residential development along M-22.

Chippewa Run is a groundwater-fed stream that flows a mile west into South Bar Lake and is named for the Anishinaabek tribes – or Chippewa Indians – who staged seasonal hunting and fishing encampments along it. Early settlers cleared much of the land and planted orchards on both sides of the creek. Eventually, the tract became known as the "Gateway to Empire" and when it was at risk of becoming a housing development the Leelanau Conservancy led a successful campaign to purchase the area. Chippewa Run Natural Area was dedicated in 2000.

Since then, conservancy volunteers have recorded nearly 80 species of birds at Chippewa Run. They range from American bitterns, great blue herons and wild turkeys to grasshopper sparrows and Eastern meadowlarks in the meadows, northern waterthrushes and Wilson's warblers in the thickets and a variety of waterfowl in the ponds and wetlands. At the south end of the preserve, green herons nest in the pines.

Much of the trail system was built in 2007-08 and today is a pair of separate loops that total less than 1.5 miles. Though it is short, the scenery is interesting and includes a variety of wildflowers, blue flag iris, cardinal flower and water lilies among them. There are excellent fall colors along the creek and old apple trees that still bear fruit. The gentle terrain makes the preserve conducive to snowshoeing and Nordic skiing in the winter.

Created in the 1960s, Chippewa Run's beaver pond hosted an active beaver community for years (photo by kenscottphotography.com).

Access and Information

From M-72 in Empire, head north on M-22. In less than a mile Chippewa Run is posted on the west side of the state highway where there is parking and a trailhead for the Orchard Loop. Across the road is the start of the Beaver Pond Loop. In winter, if the parking lot on M-22 is not plowed, turn onto LaCore Street near the Empire Area Museum and within a third of a mile, east on Fisher Street. There is a trailhead at the recycling area at the end of Fisher Street. For more information, contact the Leelanau Conservancy (231-256-9665; *leelanauconservancy.org*).

On The Trail

From the main trailhead on M-22, two trails depart into the open field — Fisher Street Access Trail to the west and Creek Crossing Trail to the north. Creek Crossing begins by skirting a wetland that includes Chippewa Run and arrives at a small pond loaded with horsetail reeds and a pair of benches that overlook it. A property owner created the pond in the 1960s and for years it hosted an active beaver community.

From the benches, the trail crosses Chippewa Run via a foot bridge and merges into Orchard Loop on the edge of the old apple orchards on the other side of the creek. Bear right and the trail ascends gently into a red pine plantation as a wide path before swinging west and heading back to the orchards. Even though many trees are gone, the patterned rows of an apple orchard are still evident.

At **Mile 0.46** you pass the junction with the Crossover Trail and then arrive again at the meandering Chippewa Run, set in a small forested ravine of native dogwood, black cherry, ash, maple, and poplar. On the other side of the creek, a stairway leads up to the Village of Empire's North Park. The trail skirts the edge of the stream corridor for a short distance, passing some huge maples along the way, and then swings east to return to the open orchard again.

At **Mile 0.9**, you arrive at the junction and the bridge over Chippewa Run and backtrack to the trailhead. To add another quarter mile to your walk, cross M-22 for the Beaver Pond Loop that begins by skirting a cattail-choked marsh to a large, open pond. At this point the trail climbs a red pine-forested ridge, topping off at a bench with a view of view of the pond below. You then follow the ridge back to M-22.

Birding Along M-22

The large amount of public land, diverse habitat and miles of shoreline and wetlands near M-22 make the state highway a birder's paradise, particularly during spring and fall migrations.

In 2013, this exceptional migratory flyway was organized as the Sleeping Bear Birding Trail (SBBT). This "trail" highlights public access to birding areas and provides interpretive signage at many trailheads. The SBBT begins at Michigan Audubon's Lake Bluff Bird Sanctuary just north of Manistee and includes the entire 116-mile route of M-22.

Chippewa Run Natural Area is among the preserves that the SBBT highlights as an excellent birding destination. While seasonal sightings and flyovers may range from bald eagles and common loons to great horned owls, species that are more commonly seen by observant hikers include:

Downy woodpecker	Hairy woodpecker	Northern flicker
Least flycatcher	Eastern phoebe	Great-crested flycatcher
Eastern kingbird	Red-eyed vireo	Blue jay
Eastern bluebird	Yellow warbler	American redstart
Scarlet tanager	Indigo bunting	Rose-breasted grosbeak
Baltimore oriole	American goldfinch	Tufted titmouse

For a data base of birding areas near the state highway and lists of species that are frequently seen at each one, go to the excellent Sleeping Bear Birding Trail website (*sleepingbearbirdingtrail.org*).

A hiker pauses along the wetland boardwalk in the middle of Swanson Preserve.

Swanson
Preserve

Swanson
Distance: 0.72 miles
Hiking Time: 1 hour
Difficulty: Easy
Highlights: Little Traverse Lake, Working farm
Map Source: Swanson Preserve from MichiganTrailMaps.com or Leelanau Conservancy at leelanauconservancy.org
Trailhead: **GPS** N44° 55' 15.31" W85° 49' 26.91"

Farm stands are a common sight along M-22 but none have been such an enduring sign of fresh produce as the pale yellow roadside stand near Little Traverse Lake. For more than a half century, Sonny Swanson stocked that hut with strawberries, sweet corn, tomatoes, pumpkins and whatever else he nurtured from the rich soil of his adjacent farm and in the process became one of the most beloved farmers on the Leelanau Peninsula.

Swanson died in 2008 at age 89 and a year later the Leelanau Conservancy was already committed to preserving the farm and one of the largest stretches of undeveloped shoreline remaining along Little Traverse Lake. The fundraising effort resulted in the conservancy purchasing 96 acres from Swanson's sons in 2010.

Within that tract, Swanson Preserve covers 83 acres including more than 2,000 feet of natural wooded shoreline near the east end of Little Traverse Lake — the fragile wetlands that are critical to the lake's high water quality — and a 162-foot high forested ridge on the south side of M-22. Most of the preserve is heavily wooded and open to the public. Access is primarily from a short trail system that leads through woods and wetlands to the shores of the Little Traverse Lake.

The other goal of the conservancy was to return Swanson's 13-acre farmstead to agricultural production. In 2011, a three-year lease was granted to Ben Brown to raise pastured poultry, pork, eggs, vegetables and flowers. On completion of the lease, Brown exercised his option to purchase the farm, which is now privately owned and not open to the public but protected against future development by a conservation easement.

Today, visitors to Swanson Preserve can enjoy a short hike to a stunningly beautiful lake and then, like summers past, stop at the familiar yellow roadside stand to see what was picked that morning.

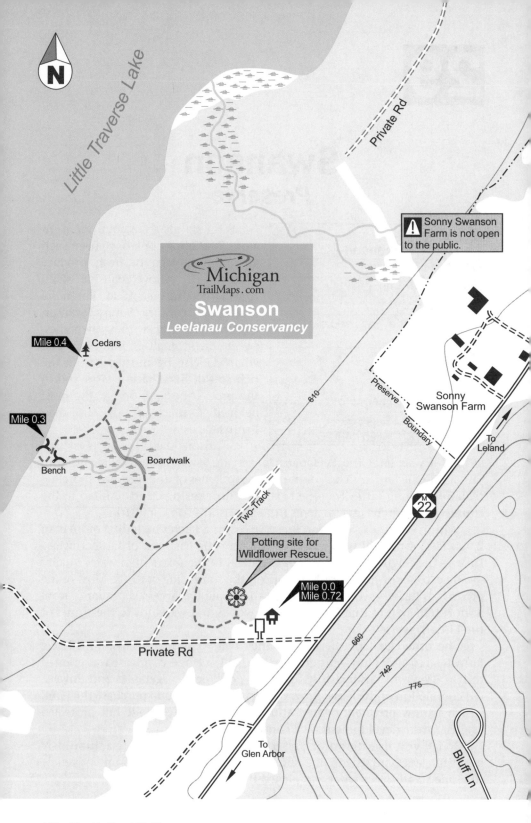

N

Little Traverse Lake

Private Rd

⚠ Sonny Swanson Farm is not open to the public.

Michigan
TrailMaps.com
Swanson
Leelanau Conservancy

Mile 0.4 ⚑ Cedars

Mile 0.3

Bench

Boardwalk

610

Preserve Boundary

Sonny Swanson Farm

To Leland

M-22

Two-Track

Potting site for Wildflower Rescue.

Mile 0.0
Mile 0.72

660

Private Rd

742

775

To Glen Arbor

Bluff Ln

Swanson Preserve includes Ben Brown's 13-acre farmstead known today at "Sonny's Farm." The privately owned farm is not open to the public.

Access and Information

Swanson Preserve is along M-22, 8 miles south of Leland or 11 miles northeast of Glen Arbor. The trailhead with parking is a posted gravel driveway about 300 yards south of the yellow farm stand.

For more information, contact the Leelanau Conservancy (231-256-9665; *leelanauconservancy.org*) or Sonny's Farm (847-271-6002; *www.sonnyswansonfarm.com*).

On The Trail

The gravel parking area for Swanson Preserve is on the edge of an open field, where a foot path enters the woods and immediately arrives at the potting site for Wildflower Rescue. A volunteer-based arm of the Leelanau Conservancy, the Wildflower Rescue Committee was started in 1999 with the intent to save native plants from the construction of roads, buildings, homes and other development. Plants are removed, potted and then donated to public gardens or sold to raise funds for the conservancy.

Just beyond the potting site the trail crosses an old two-track and in less than quarter mile from the trailhead arrives at a boardwalk. The planking keeps the boots dry as you cross a stream and pass through a wetland area of seeps and springs, all feeding into Little Traverse Lake. Just beyond the boardwalk is a posted junction to a pair of short spurs to the lake.

Head left and you'll briefly skirt an unnamed stream and arrive at a bench overlooking Little Traverse Lake at *Mile 0.3*. It's less than 200 yards to the end of the other spur, a beautiful spot on the lake where a grove of tilted white cedars grace the shoreline.

Backtrack to the junction and then across the boardwalk to reach the trailhead at *Mile 0.72*.

Sonny Swanson's Roadside Stand

In the 1920s Robert and Ruthella Swanson purchased a farm along M-22, raised four children and in 1931 built a roadside stand to sell their produce to locals and the growing number of motorists passing by. Eventually, the two sons inherited the farm but it was Sonny Swanson who picked up where his parents left off. Sonny and his wife lived in Traverse City so he commuted daily to his fields to manage the crops and stock the counter and shelves of what was now the farm's landmark produce stand.

During the summer, the hut was laden with strawberries, radishes, corn, tomatoes and whatever else Sonny coaxed from the ground. In the fall, it overflowed with pumpkins and squash. When Sonny was at the stand he enjoyed socializing with customers and enticing them with free samples to try something new. When he wasn't at the stand, there was an honesty box for payment, with a hand-lettered sign reading: "God knows everything. Thank you for being honest."

For 50 years, Sonny's stand was always yellow and the farmer was always nearby. The hut has been such an iconic part of the Leelanau Peninsula that it was once the topic of a New York Times column and in 1999 was featured on the poster for the Manitou Music Festival.

After Sonny's death in 2008, the shelves sat empty for three summers. But in a testimony to one farmer's legacy, a movement to preserve the farm and a way of life in northern Michigan resulted in Sonny's Stand reopening in 2011.

Teichner
Preserve

Teichner	
Distance: 0.4 miles	
Hiking Time: 30 minutes	
Difficulty: Easy	
Highlights: Lime Lake, Wetland boardwalk	
Map Source: Teichner Preserve from MichiganTrailMaps.com or Leelanau Conservancy at leelanauconservancy.org	
Trailhead: GPS N44° 54' 12.98" W85° 49' 41.84"	

In 1977, Martha Teichner joined CBS News and filed her first story with legendary Walter Cronkite sitting at the anchor desk and since then has reported the news from across the world.

She covered Britain's royal wedding of Prince Charles to Lady Diana Spencer as well as Princess Diana's death. Teichner was part of a small group of journalists allowed by the military to accompany U.S. troops during the Persian Gulf War, reported on the fall of Communism in Central and Eastern Europe, was there when Nelson Mandela was released from prison and then covered his election when he became the first black president of post-apartheid South Africa.

The winner of nine Emmy Awards and five James Beard Broadcast Awards is based in New York City as a correspondent for "CBS Sunday Morning," but the shores of Lime Lake in Leelanau County are always in her heart. Teichner was born in Traverse City and for 10 years lived with her family on the Lime Lake's northeast shore in the shadow of Sugar Loaf Mountain, where her father was a ski instructor.

In 1996, the news correspondent donated her family's 20 acres near the lake to the Leelanau Conservancy in memory of her parents and Teichner Preserve was established. Ten years later Teichner was in northern Michigan when she learned that within two weeks a nine-acre waterfront parcel near the preserve was slated to be cleared for residential development.

Teichner contacted the Leelanau Conservancy, which worked with the landowner to negotiate a purchase price. She then refinanced the mortgage on her New York apartment and used $200,000 of it to cover more than half of the purchase price. It was Teichner's second gift to the conservancy in a decade.

Such generosity prompted a neighboring landowner, Jean Raymond, to donate eight acres between the original preserve and the waterfront property.

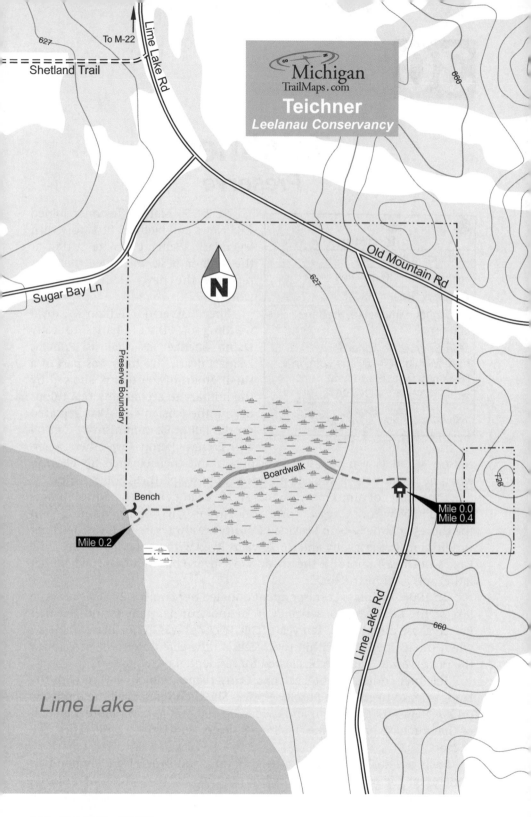

627

To M-22

Shetland Trail

660

Michigan
TrailMaps.com
Teichner
Leelanau Conservancy

Old Mountain Rd

627

N

Sugar Bay Ln

Preserve Boundary

726

Boardwalk

Mile 0.0
Mile 0.4

Bench

Mile 0.2

660

Lime Lake

Today, Teichner Preserve has 41 acres, includes 200 feet of undeveloped shoreline on Lime Lake and forested wetlands that contain giant elms and chestnuts, rare trees most likely planted by early settlers.

The preserve might be small and the trail short — a mere half mile to the lake and back — but the area is blessed with the natural beauty of the wetlands and infused with the passion of those who were so determined to save it.

Access and Information

From Leland, head south on M-22 for 9.5 miles and turn left on Lime Lake Road. Within a mile is the posted trailhead of Teichner Preserve on the west side of Lime Lake Road. For more information contact the Leelanau Conservancy (231-256-9665; *leelanauconservancy.org*). The conservancy also has an office in Leland at 105 North First St. that is open Monday through Friday from 8:30 a.m. to 5 p.m.

On The Trail

There are no facilities at the trailhead other than parking for a handful of vehicles. The trail descends from the parking area past an information display to a former road that once extended to the lake. Eventually, the road and its fill pad were removed and the wetland restored to allow its natural flow to again filter the waters of Lime Lake.

Within 100 yards a boardwalk leads you through the forested wetland that is the heart of Teichner Preserve. Along with the enormous elm and chestnut trees, the swampy lowlands are home to black ash, ironwood and red maple while white ash and sugar maple grow in surrounding upland areas. Observant hikers might also spot several rare species of ferns, including rattlesnake, interrupted, and maindenhair. Blue flag iris can be spotted in the marsh while the most common wildlife encountered are woodcock, grouse and wild turkeys.

The boardwalk gives way to a foot path that quickly leads to a bench in a tangle of tamarack and cedar near the shoreline. In the fall, the tamarack's needles turn a golden yellow to blend in beautifully with the colors of the surrounding hardwoods. The view of Lime Lake from the bench is worthy of a long break even though you've hiked less than a quarter mile. Backtrack the boardwalk to return to the trailhead.

The boardwalk at sunset in Teichner Preserve (photo by kenscottphotography.com).

Hans "Peppi" Teichner, a Legend of His Own

As fascinating as Martha Teichner's career has been, equally compelling is the life story of her father, Hans "Peppi" Teichner, often regarded as the father of skiing in Michigan's Lower Peninsula. Born in Plauen, Germany in 1908, Peppi was a Jewish member of Germany's national ski team when Adolph Hitler rose to power, prompting him to move to Spain in 1933 to coach the Spanish Olympic Team.

Hans "Peppi" Teichner (photo courtesy of U.S. Ski & Snowboard Hall of Fame).

When the Spanish Civil War broke out in 1936, Peppi organized "ski classes" as a way to guide Spanish Loyalists and others fleeing Francisco Franco's fascist regime across the Pyrenees Mountains to France. Legend has it that a patrol once spotted him, but Peppi managed to out-ski his would-be captors. Now a wanted man, he narrowly escaped capture by Franco's fascists on his flight to safety in France.

In 1937, he sought haven in the United States and was a ski instructor at Sun Valley when World War II broke out. Peppi went on to become a member of the famed 10th Mountain Division, serving as one of the first ski and rock climbing instructors for the army.

After the war Peppi joined other members of the 10th Mountain Division at the new downhill ski resort at Aspen, Colo., before moving to Michigan and settling in Leelanau County. A friend from the 10th Mountain Division convinced him to help create a local downhill area and in 1948 the Sugar Loaf Winter Sports Club opened with a tow rope rigged up to a tractor engine. Eventually, the downhill area became Sugar Loaf Mountain.

Peppi was also instrumental in the establishment of the Holiday Hills and Hickory Hills ski areas in Traverse City and, as a teacher at Leelanau School, worked to help downhill skiing become an interscholastic sport in Michigan.

But he is best remembered as a longtime instructor who taught a region to ski, with students ranging from Michigan First Lady Helen Milliken to children with disabilities. One of Peppi's students was Jean Raymond, whose eight-acre donation in 2005, completed Teichner Preserve. Peppi died in 1957 at age 49, and in 1967 was inducted into the U.S. Ski & Snowboard Hall of Fame in Ishpeming.

The observation deck at Whaleback Natural Area (photo by kenscottphotography.com).

31

Whaleback
Natural Area

Whaleback	
Distance: 1.6 miles	
Hiking Time: 1 hour	
Difficulty: Moderate	
Highlights: Hardwood bluff, Lake Michigan views	
Map Source: Whaleback Natural Area from MichiganTrailMaps.com or Leelanau Conservancy at leelanauconservancy.org	
Trailhead: **GPS** N45°0' 22.21" W85° 46' 11.63"	

On U.S. Geological Survey topographical maps, Leelanau County's most noted landmark is labeled Carp River Point. To everybody else, the distinctive point that juts into Lake Michigan just south of Leland looks more like a whale than a carp.

The bluff known as Whaleback catches the attention of anyone scanning Lake Michigan from afar. To many, the distinctive ridge looks like a beached whale, one they can spot while standing in Leland's Fishtown, from a high point in northern Leelanau County or from several beaches in the area, particularly Good Harbor Bay, which the point encloses to the north. Encompassing 117 acres and 3,700 feet of lakeshore, Whaleback towers 300 feet above Lake Michigan and has long been used by sailors as a point of reference.

This whale is actually a moraine. Formed by a glacier 11,000 years ago, Whaleback is, in geologist terms, a "drumlin," a long, oval mound of glacial drift that was molded in the same direction as the original flow of ice. What was left behind was a geologic wonder with spectacular views from the edge of its steep-sided ridge and a terrain supporting a variety of plants and wildlife, all within a five-minute drive or less from one of Northern Michigan's most popular tourist towns.

Whaleback had to be preserved. In 1996, the Leelanau Conservancy completed the task when it raised $850,000 to acquire 40 acres of the coastal bluff and rocky beach at its base. Whaleback Natural Area was open to the public after the conservancy worked with surrounding landowners to develop a trail across private property to the preserve. The natural area is small and the trail system limited, with not much more than a mile of paths.

The views of the lake are what attract most hikers to Whaleback but the flora can also be fascinating. In the spring, the forest is covered by vast swaths of wildflowers such as trillium and columbine. In the fall, hardwoods create a colorful canopy above the trail. Whaleback's most unusual resident is the

Lake Michigan

Michigan
TrailMaps.com
Whaleback
Leelanau Conservancy

Mile 0.8

Birch
Valley
Trail

⚠ This is a private
trail off the bluff.

Bluff Edge Trail

858

742

Manitou
Lookout
Loop

▲ 881 ft

Mile 0.5

Viewing
Deck

825

776

Oxford Dr

Whaleback Mountain Rd

N

Mile 0.4
Mile 1.2

Glacial Hill Trail

Bench

825

742

660

594

660

627

To Leland

Mile 0.0
Mile 1.6

Good Harbor Bay

⚠ From the trailhead
Glacial Hill Trail passes
through private property for
0.3 mile before entering the
preserve. Please stay on the
the trail during that stretch.

Private Drive

M 22

To
Glen Arbor

Lake Leelanau

thimbleberry, a large raspberry-like fruit that is common along Lake Superior in the western Upper Peninsula but rarely seen in the Lower Peninsula.

The trails at Whaleback can be combined for a 1.6-mile hike from the trailhead off M-22. The distances are short but the climb up to the top of the bluff is steady, making the natural area a moderately challenging outing. In the winter, Whaleback is a better destination for snowshoeing than backcountry skiing as the initial incline leaves most skiers looking elsewhere.

Access and Information

From the junction of M-22 and M-204, head north on M-22 for a mile. A natural area sign on the west (left) side of M-22 marks a private gravel drive that leads 200 yards west to the Whaleback trailhead and parking area. Whaleback is less than 1.5 miles from the heart of Leland, but if driving south from the town the Leelanau Conservancy sign can be difficult to spot.

For more information, contact the Leelanau Conservancy (231-256-9665; *leelanauconservancy.org*).

On The Trail

At the trailhead, there is parking for a handful of cars and an information kiosk. Glacial Hill Trail, the access trail, enters the woods and begins its steady upward march. It's not steep but it is a continuous climb of almost a half mile. The access trail passes through private property for a third of a mile before entering the preserve, so it is important to stay on the designated path during that stretch. Within a quarter mile is a bench overlooking a vineyard, a pleasant place to take a break.

A sign indicates you have entered the natural area, followed by a junction of the return of Manitou Lookout Loop (stay left) and then views of Lake Michigan through the trees before you reach the short spur to the observation deck. Reached at *Mile 0.5*, the platform is perched on the edge of the glacial moraine and equipped with benches. For the price of a climb, you're rewarded a spectacular view of the green-blue waters of Good Harbor Bay below, Pyramid Point due west and the Manitou Islands on the horizon.

The main trail continues to hug the edge of the bluff, providing glimpses of Lake Michigan through the trees. Continuing in a northerly direction, it's along this stretch that those with sharp eyes will spot the patches of thimbleberries. Two junctions are passed within a quarter mile (stay left) before the trail descends to a point reached at *Mile 0.8*. Here is a view of the shoreline leading to the village of Leland, Lake Leelanau and a sign that reads "Private Beyond," reminding you how small the natural area is.

The loop known as Birch Valley Trail swings south and passes a posted junction with a private trail that descends a ravine off the bluff. The conservancy trail heads right. You backtrack briefly and then head left at the junction of Manitou Lookout Loop passed earlier to arrive at Glacial Hill Trail at *Mile 1.2*. Backtrack the access trail, a much more enjoyable walk the second time around, heading downhill to the trailhead.

Hikers are greeted with a view of Lake Michigan at Clay Cliffs Natural Area.

32

Clay Cliffs
Natural Area

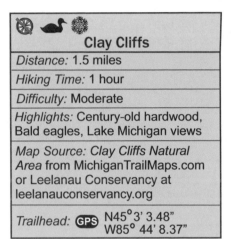

Clay Cliffs

Distance: 1.5 miles	
Hiking Time: 1 hour	
Difficulty: Moderate	
Highlights: Century-old hardwood, Bald eagles, Lake Michigan views	
Map Source: Clay Cliffs Natural Area from MichiganTrailMaps.com or Leelanau Conservancy at leelanauconservancy.org	
Trailhead: **GPS** N45° 3' 3.48" W85° 44' 8.37"	

The trail system at Clay Cliffs Natural Area totals less than 1.6 miles, yet in that short distance hikers skirt towering bluffs, pass two stunning panoramas and in the spring are greeted by a palette of wildflowers. This is 104.5 acres everybody wanted to protect from development, including its owner.

Wedged between Lake Michigan and Lake Leelanau, Clay Cliffs was one of Leelanau County's largest privately owned coastal property when owner Doug Crary and the Leelanau Conservancy began discussing how to preserve it in the early 1990s. Teaming up with Leland Township in 2010, the conservancy oversaw a $5.8 million fundraiser that included a Michigan Natural Resources Trust Fund grant, a sizeable contribution from the Crary family and generous donations from locals. In 2013, Clay Cliffs was dedicated as a Leland Township natural area to be managed by the conservancy.

The Cliffs are a rare clay bluff ecosystem, a forested drumlin sculptured by glaciers and later waves, resulting in 200-foot near-vertical clay slopes that rise dramatically above Lake Michigan. A portion of the area was once farmed, so today the preserve is a mix of century-old hardwoods, cleared hayfields, open meadows and wetland seeps fed by springs.

Its topography, ranging from the clay cliffs and hidden valleys to 3,500 feet of shoreline split between Lake Michigan and Lake Leelanau, provide a diverse habitat for wildflowers and wildlife. Clay Cliffs is one of the most prolific wildflower sites in Leelanau County — particularly trilliums in the spring — with its most noted residents a pair of nesting bald eagles.

The preserve's trail system, along with a trailhead parking area and an observation deck perched over the edge of the cliff, was built in 2014-15 and is basically a loop with a crossover spur. Though the perimeter of the system is only 1.5 miles, this hike involves a steady climb of almost 150 feet in elevation and an almost equally long descent. For this reason snowshoes

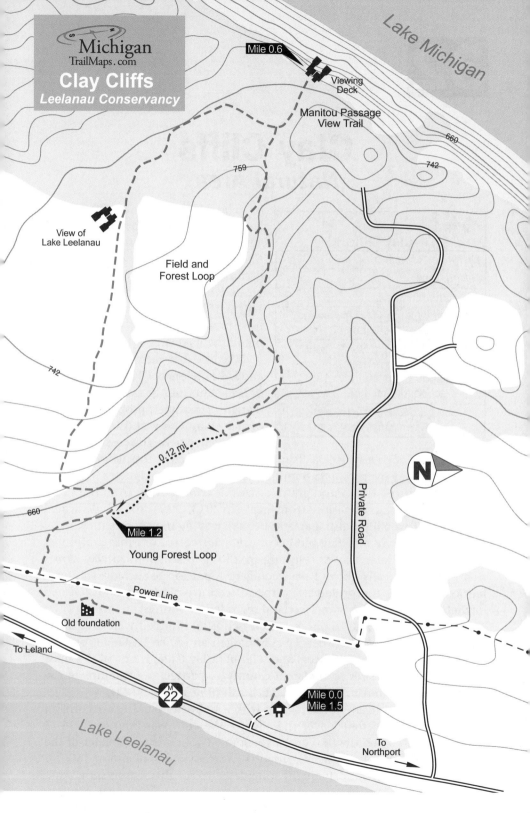

Lake Michigan

Michigan
TrailMaps.com
Clay Cliffs
Leelanau Conservancy

Mile 0.6

Viewing
Deck

Manitou Passage
View Trail

660

742

759

View of
Lake Leelanau

Field and
Forest Loop

742

0.12 mi.

660

N

Mile 1.2

Young Forest Loop

Private Road

Power Line

Old foundation

To Leland

M 22

Mile 0.0
Mile 1.5

To
Northport

Lake Leelanau

are preferred in the winter over backcountry skis.

Access and Information ─────────────────────────

Clay Cliffs Natural Area is posted along M-22, 2.5 miles north of the village of Leland. For more information, contact the Leelanau Conservancy (231-256-9665; *leelanauconservancy.org*) or stop at the conservancy office, 105 North First St., in Leland. The office is open 8:30 a.m. to 5 p.m. Monday through Friday.

On The Trail ────────────────────────────────

The trailhead at Clay Cliffs features a parking area capable of holding a dozen vehicles and an information kiosk but no source of drinking water or toilets. The Young Forest Loop departs west and quickly comes to a junction where continuing west (right) is a path that was constructed in 2015. This segment passes under a power line, skirts a small meadow and arrives at a junction with the Field and Forest Loop. Head right to continue on the loop and prepare for a steady climb through a mature northern hardwood forest.

In the next third of a mile there is a gain of 149 feet in elevation, reaching the high point of the trail, 759 feet, just before reaching the short spur, dubbed Manitou Passage View Trail, to the observation deck. The impressive wooden structure is reached at *Mile 0.6* and allows you to stand over the edge of the steep cliff comprised of clay lenses, sand and gravel. The view is magnificent, with the most prominent landmarks being North Manitou Island, whose southern tip is only 10 miles due west, and the perched dunes of Pyramid Point to the southwest. Between the two is South Manitou Island; to the northwest is South Fox Island.

Backtrack to the Field and Forest Loop and head right to briefly skirt the cliffs — other than winter the hardwoods prevent a view of Lake Michigan from the trail. You then swing more due east and at *Mile 1* break out into a large rye field where you are greeted with a view of Lake Leelanau surrounded by ridges, orchards and vineyards.

It's classic Leelanau. The view remains until the trail enters the woods and makes a steady descent, including a switchback, bottoming out at the junction with the Young Forest Loop, reached at *Mile 1.2*.

Head right to continue on a wide trail that swings close enough to M-22 to hear the traffic. It also passes the rock walls of a Michigan basement, all that remains of the farmhouse that once stood there, before arriving at the trailhead at *Mile 1.5*.

Hikers enjoying Houdek Dunes Natural Area in early spring.

Houdek Dunes
Natural Area

Houdek Dunes
Distance: 2.95 miles
Hiking Time: 2 hours
Difficulty: Moderate
Highlights: Giant white birch trees, Open dunes, Trout stream
Map Source: Houdek Dunes Natural Area from MichiganTrailMaps.com or Leelanau Conservancy at leelanauconservancy.org
Trailhead: **GPS** N45° 4' 6.06" W85° 41' 31.82"

The trail at Houdek Dunes Natural Area begins with a long wooden stairway. Within 30 steps from the trailhead, you leave behind the traffic zipping along on M-22 and enter a stand of quaking aspen, whose leaves gently spin with every light breeze.

There is also a bench here. Take a break even though it's the start of your hike and soak in the serenity of this special place. In the middle of summer you have already escaped the tourist season.

At 342 acres, Houdek Dunes is one of Leelanau Conservancy's largest and most diverse preserves. The landscape ranges from hardwood forests featuring some of the largest white birch trees in northern Michigan to Houdek Creek, a spring-fed trout stream and the primary tributary flowing into northern Lake Leelanau. Then there are dunes. These mounds of sand are the result of glacial sediments being exposed 4,000 years ago when the ancient Lake Nippissing receded. The trails skirt active blowout dunes, cross stretches of open sand scattered with tracks and climb forested backdunes with views of hardwoods below.

Stretching a quarter mile inland from Lake Michigan, the dunes form a barrier between Houdek Creek and upland hardwood forests of aspen and red oak along with beech and maple in the sheltered valleys. The woodland pockets, created by dips in the dunes, are also responsible for Houdek's most stunning trees: large, healthy white birches. Thriving in the narrow ravines and hollows that shield them from the wind, many of the birches are more than a century old, an age that is highly unusual for this transitional species.

The land were logged more than a century ago and then farmed by the Houdek family. The agricultural past is evident today as remnant apple trees from orchards long gone and fence posts that indicate cattle grazing. Eventually, the area was destined to become another golf course when the Leelanau Conservancy staged a campaign to acquire the tract in 1998 including a mile of frontage on M-22 and 4,500 feet along Houdek Creek.

The trail system at Houdek Dunes totals 3.5 miles, including three

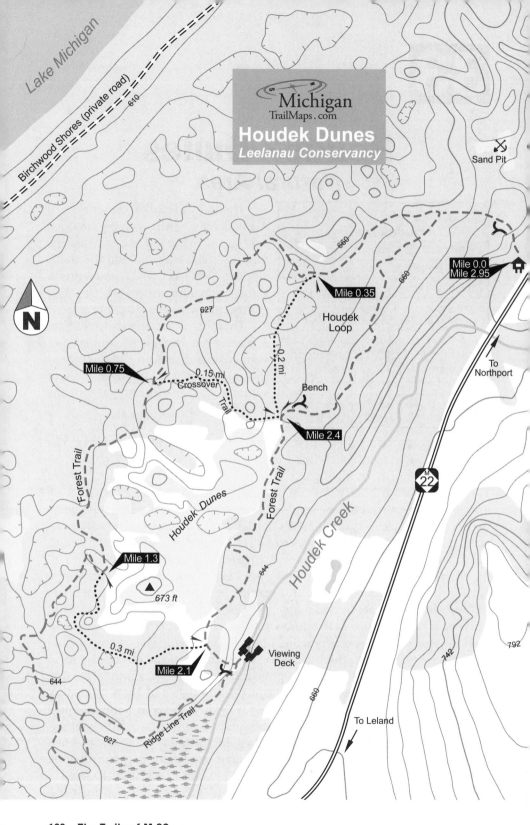

Lake Michigan

Birchwood Shores (private road)

610

Michigan
TrailMaps.com
Houdek Dunes
Leelanau Conservancy

Sand Pit

660

660

Mile 0.0
Mile 2.95

Mile 0.35

Houdek
Loop

627

N

Mile 0.75

0.15 mi
Crossover
Trail

0.2 mi

To
Northport

Bench

Mile 2.4

Forest Trail

Forest Trail

Houdek Dunes

Houdek Creek

M 22

Mile 1.3

644

▲
673 ft

0.3 mi

Mile 2.1

Viewing
Deck

644

660

742

792

627

Ridge Line Trail

To Leland

crossover spurs, with the perimeter trails forming a loop of nearly 3 miles. The hiking is considered easy to moderate due to soft sand and a few moderately steep slopes. In the winter, Houdek Dunes is a favorite among cross-country skiers looking for a backcountry challenge on ungroomed trails.

Access and Information

From Leland, head north on M-22 and in 5 miles, or almost a mile past County Road 626, Houdek Dunes is posted on the left. For more information, contact the Leelanau Conservancy (231-256-9665; *leelanauconservancy.org*) or stop at the conservancy office, 105 North First St., in Leland.

On The Trail

Like most Leelanau Conservancy preserves, the Houdek Dunes trailhead has a small parking lot and an information kiosk but no source of drinking water or toilets. The trail begins with that stairway and then continues through a rolling forested terrain. Within a few hundred yards is the junction with the return of the Houdek Loop Trail, the first loop of the system and a hike of less than a mile. To continue on the perimeter, head right.

The bulk of the hike is along the Forest Trail, which is reached at the second junction at *Mile 0.35* and begins in a lightly forested area of rolling dunes. Within a quarter mile the trail begins a steady climb that tops off just beyond the junction with the Crossover Trail at *Mile 0.75*. You dip and climb through forested terrain reaching the next junction at *Mile 1.3*, with the Forest Trail continuing south (left). Head west (right) along the Ridge Line Trail, skirting wooded hollows from above and climbing to the top of a small knoll. At 660 feet, or 76 feet above Lake Michigan, this is the highest point along the loop, high enough to provide a view of other parts of the preserve and a vineyard clinging to the side of a ridge in the distance.

The trail immediately descends off the knob and continues along grassy ridgelines that allows for glimpses into more hollows and pockets of impressive birch trees. At *Mile 2*, Ridge Line Trail arrives at a posted junction and an octagon-shaped viewing deck that was built and donated by the Houdek Family. The view includes serene Houdek Creek gently flowing past an embankment of grassy and open dunes. Nearby is a bench under a tree overlooking the creek, a soothing spot for an extended break or lunch.

The short Houdek Creek Trail heads west and to return to the Forest Trail on the edge of the preserve's most impressive dunes. Head north (right) and soon the trail is traversing a fine line with open dunes on one side and trees on the other. At one point, blue-tipped posts lead across open sand — on the other side you enter the forest for good and at *Mile 2.4* arrive at a junction with Crossover Trail and Houdek Loop Trail. Nearby, a pair of benches are positioned in front of the "ancient maple," a large, old and distinctively gnarly tree, looking like it belongs in the Wizard of Oz Haunted Forest.

Follow the Houdek Loop Trail, a level path through the woods, and in a half mile you'll be back at the trailhead stairway.

Wildflowers near the shore of Kehl Lake (photo by kenscottphotography.com).

34

Kehl Lake
Natural Area

Kehl Lake	
Distance: 2.1 miles	
Hiking Time: 1 hour	
Difficulty: Easy	
Highlights: Kehl Lake, Old-growth white pines	
Map Source: Kehl Lake Natural Area from MichiganTrailMaps.com or Leelanau Conservancy at leelanauconservancy.org	
Trailhead: **GPS** N45° 10' 11,21" W85° 35' 45.68"	

The 279-acre Kehl Lake Natural Area north of Northport features 2,500 feet of undeveloped shoreline along the 74-acre lake, paths that wander through extensive hardwood-conifer swamps and excellent birding, including opportunities to spot a blue-headed vireo or Blackburnian warbler. But in the end, what commands your attention are the trees.

For many visitors, the most impressive sights are above them — mature white pines and towering hemlocks whose needles and branches reach for the sky. Even the preserve's "Old Birch," whose branches haven't sprouted foliage in years, makes one pause and wonder at its massive trunk.

The lake and the trees first captured the attention of Ottawa and Chippewa tribes who used the area for seasonal settlements and called it "Medahas-ah-eegan" or Leg Lake, a name still seen on maps today. In the 1860s, John and Elizabeth Kehl arrived from Buffalo, N.Y., built a cabin and farmed a 160-acre homestead along the southern half of the lake. Eventually, Leg Lake became known as Kehl Lake.

But much of the area, a mixture of wetlands and lowland hardwoods and conifers surrounded by poorly drained soils, was not well suited for farming, so it was never disturbed. What attracted the Leelanau Conservancy were mature, large trees of various species and the importance of Kehl Lake as part of a wildlife corridor that spans across the tip of the Leelanau Peninsula, from Northport Bay to Cathead Bay, and Cathead Point to Lighthouse Point. Following the conservancy's original purchase of 113 acres of the Kehl Farm in 1990, the preserve has been expanded three times to its current size in an effort to protect a corridor that includes three other conservancy parcels and Leelanau State Park.

Though some eastern white pines are estimated to be more than a century old, the trees are not the old-growth giants seen elsewhere in Michigan as fluctuating water conditions never allowed any one species to dominate.

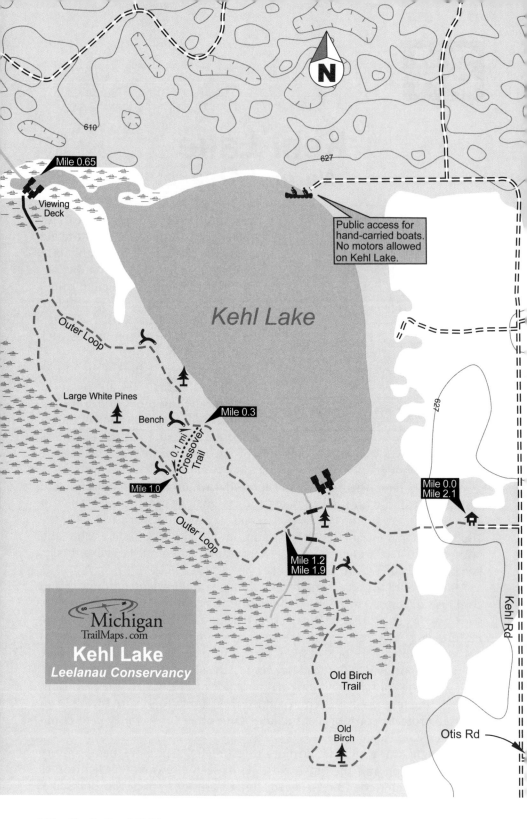

Kehl Lake

Mile 0.65

Viewing Deck

610

627

Public access for hand-carried boats. No motors allowed on Kehl Lake.

Outer Loop

Large White Pines

Bench

Mile 0.3

0.1 mi Crossover Trail

Mile 1.0

Outer Loop

629

Mile 0.0
Mile 2.1

Mile 1.2
Mile 1.9

Michigan
TrailMaps.com
Kehl Lake
Leelanau Conservancy

Old Birch Trail

Old Birch

Kehl Rd

Otis Rd

The older white pines are 100 feet to 120 feet in height and feature huge trunks often three feet to four feet in diameter. Other species of impressive size include white cedar, hemlock, black spruce, beech, paper birch and sugar maple.

The trail system at Kehl Lake includes two loops: the 1.4-mile Outer Loop and the 0.7-mile Birch Loop, with connecting trails and a crossover spur. The entire system, including a trail to the observation deck on the lake, makes for an easy 2.1-mile hike along paths that are level and surprisingly dry considering the wetlands they skirt. In the winter, the preserve's gentle terrain is popular with cross-country skiers.

Access and Information

From M-22, head north on M-201 through downtown Northport and then continue after the state highway becomes County Road 640 (Woolsey Lake Rd). Within 2.5 miles of Northport, turn north (left) on Snyder Road and then east (right) on Sugar Bush Road. Sugar Bush takes a sharp left turn to the north and becomes Kehl Road. Stay on Kehl and within 0.7 miles, or a quarter mile past Otis Road, is the posted entrance to Kehl Lake Natural Area on the left.

For more information, contact the Leelanau Conservancy (231-256-9665; *leelanauconservancy.org*) or stop at the conservancy office, 105 North First St., in Leland.

On The Trail

Most of the year the footing over the 2.1 miles is dry but in early spring snow can linger in the woods and parts of the trail can be flooded with runoff.

From the trailhead, the trail passes through a small meadow and then enters the woods to quickly arrive at the south end of Kehl Lake. The lack of development, ban on boat motors and the surrounding wetlands has resulted in the lake's exceptional water quality and clarity. You can't launch a boat at the natural area but canoes and other hand-carried boats can be launched at a public access near the north side of the lake at the end of Kehl Road.

In less than a quarter mile you cross a bridge over a small stream feeding into Kehl Lake and arrive at the junction to the return trail from the Outer Loop. Stay right to follow the west shore of the lake. The trail provides glimpses of the water through the trees and some of those ancient white pines. Within a third of a mile you pass the junction with the Crossover Trail and at **Mile 0.4** arrive at a bench where the trail swings close to the lake.

At this point the trail swings west and shortly arrives at the spur to the observation dock. This area can be wet but the worst of it is crossed on planking that reaches the long dock at **Mile 0.65** at the north end of Kehl Lake. During spring and fall migrations, this is a great spot to hang out with a pair of binoculars.

Birding at Kehl Lake Natural Area

Winter owl (photo by Nate Richardson).

Due to a variety of habitats and close proximity to Lake Michigan at the tip of the Leelanau Peninsula, Kehl Lake is one of 35 designated sites along the Sleeping Bear Birding Trail (*sleepingbearbirdingtrail.org*). The 279-acre natural area is only a quarter mile from Cathead Bay and is used by migrating birds along the Lake Michigan Flyway as a stopover before crossing to and from the Upper Peninsula.

The lake attracts a variety of waterfowl during spring and fall migrations while in the surrounding forests birders will spot both migrating and nesting warblers and other songbirds. Among the breeding birds encountered in the preserve's lowland hardwood-conifer forest are black-billed cuckoo, olive-sided flycatcher, veery, northern parula, black-throated blue and blackburnian warblers, northern waterthrush and white-throated sparrow. Year-round residents include ruffed grouse, barred owl, and pileated woodpecker, while sandhill cranes, and in the winter, snowy owls have been spotted passing through.

Backtrack to the junction and continue following the Outer Loop to the right. The trail skirts the lowland forested wetlands but stays dry and just before the junction with the Crossover Trail at Mile 1, passes another old-growth white pine. At **Mile 1.2**, you arrive at the junction with the Old Birch Loop, which was built in 2006 and adds 0.7 miles to the hike. If followed in a clockwise direction you quickly pass a bench at the junction with the return trail and then in a third of a mile arrive at Old Birch, whose lifeless giant trunk stands as a monument to the species.

You return to the Outer Loop at **Mile 1.9** and backtrack to the trailhead and parking area.

Jeff Lamont
Preserve

Jeff Lamont	
Distance: 0.3 miles round-trip	
Hiking Time: 20 minutes	
Difficulty: Easy	
Highlights: Wildflowers including pink lady's slipper orchids	
Map Source: Jeff Lamont Preserve from MichiganTrailMaps.com or Leelanau Conservancy at leelanauconservancy.org	
Trailhead: **GPS**	N45° 9' 59.62" W85° 37' 32.17"

The Jeff Lamont Preserve was purchased by the Lamont family in 2008 and donated to the Leelanau Conservancy in honor of their son, who died at the age of 21 after a six-year battle with cancer. The Lamont family cottage is on nearby Cathead Bay and Jeff grew up exploring the woodlands and forested wetlands of this 40-acre track.

Lamont is part of a string of preserves that create a wildlife corridor across the tip of the Leelanau Peninsula and include Kehl Lake, the Cathead Bay portion of Leelanau State Park and Lighthouse West, and Finton Natural Areas. Within the heavily forested preserve are stands of old maple, beech and hemlock that allow birders to spot such canopy species as scarlet tanager and black-throated blue warbler.

The preserve's short trail skirts wetlands and even standing pools of water, something to consider during the buggy months of June and July. But in the spring and early summer the same habitat can be a colorful bouquet of woodland and wetland wildflowers, including pink lady's slippers, swamp rose, marsh marigolds, Jack-in-the-pulpit and wild columbine.

Access and Information

The Jeff Lamont Preserve is an out-of-the-way place in the woods. From M-22 in Northport, head north on M-201 and continue as it becomes County Road 640 and swings east. Within 2.2 miles from M-22, turn north (left) on Kilcherman Road, an intersection featuring a nearby antique windmill. Within a mile, Kilcherman swings sharply west (left) and becomes Christmas Cove Road. Follow Christmas Cove Road for a half mile — 250 yards after passing Scott Road is the preserve's posted trailhead on the north side of the road.

For more information about the Jeff Lamont Preserve, contact the

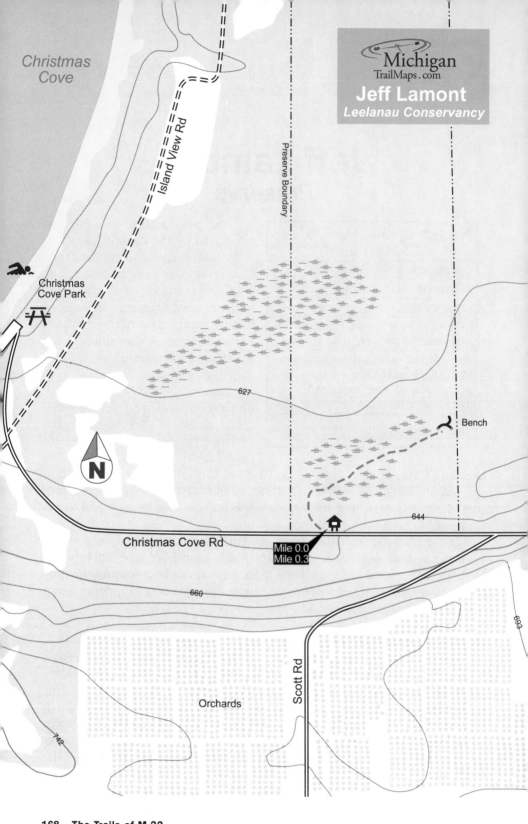

Christmas
Cove

Island View Rd

Preserve Boundary

Michigan
TrailMaps.com
Jeff Lamont
Leelanau Conservancy

Christmas
Cove Park

Bench

627

N

644

Christmas Cove Rd

Mile 0.0
Mile 0.3

660

693

Scott Rd

Orchards

742

The bench at Jeff Lamont Preserve (photo by kenscottphotography.com).

Leelanau Conservancy (231-256-9665; *leelanauconservancy.org*) or stop at the conservancy office, 105 North First St., in Leland. The office is open 8:30 a.m. to 5 p.m. Monday through Friday.

On The Trail

There are no facilities at the Lamont trailhead other than parking. But a half mile west of the trailhead, Christmas Cove Road ends at Christmas Cove Park. The Leelanau Township park includes 200 feet of Lake Michigan beach along with a picnic area and large parking area.

The Jeff Lamont Trail appears as an old two-track that swings to the east through a hardwood forest that forms a leafy tunnel over the path. Scattered pockets of wetlands appear on both sides of the trail before you reach a bench at Mile 0.15. The bench marks the end of the trail and can be a pleasant place to sit and gather your thoughts. Nearby, a "No Trespassing – Keep Out" sign is erected across the two-track, a reminder of why it's so important to protect even the smallest parcels and the shortest trails.

Glacial erratics at Lighthouse West Natural Area (photo by kenscottphotography.com).

Lighthouse West
Natural Area

⊛ 🦆 ❄
Lighthouse West
Distance: 1.3 miles
Hiking Time: 1 hour
Difficulty: Easy
Highlights: Excellent birding for songbirds and broad-winged raptors
Map Source: Lighthouse West from MichiganTrailMaps.com or Leelanau Conservancy at leelanauconservancy.org
Trailhead: **GPS** N45° 12' 19.25" W85° 32' 49.04"

Unlike its adjoining counterpart, Leelanau State Park, there is no lighthouse in Lighthouse West Natural Area. Or a campground or picnic tables or restrooms or a maritime museum.

The two parks preserve 230 acres of the tip of the Leelanau Peninsula, which includes the historic Grand Traverse Lighthouse. But the bulk of that, along with all the visitor amenities, is in the state park. The natural area is only 42 acres and 640 feet of shoreline along Lake Michigan.

But to thousands of songbirds and broad-winged raptors that migrate to nesting grounds in the Upper Peninsula and Canada, Lighthouse West is a blessing, a stopover for food and rest before crossing the wide expanse of Lake Michigan. And for birders, the natural area is a place to see more than 100 species during the spring and fall migrations.

Established in 2004, Lighthouse West is part of a 625-acre wildlife corridor the Leelanau Conservancy has pieced together across the tip of the Leelanau Peninsula, from Northport Bay to Lighthouse Point.

During the spring migration from mid-April to mid-May, the northern reach of the peninsula is one of the best birding spots in the region. Waves of birds, from warblers, tanagers and orioles to shorebirds, waders and raptors, hug the Lake Michigan shoreline and are funneled up into the Leelanau Peninsula. When foul weather sets in, the birds linger at Lighthouse West while waiting for a warm southerly breeze to guide them across the open water. Other species, including scarlet tanagers, black-billed cuckoos and chestnut-sided warblers nest in the area.

Lighthouse West features 1.2 miles of trail, built in 2009 and designed to traverse the various habitats that appeal to birds, and thus, birders. The perimeter of the system, including a segment to and from the shoreline,

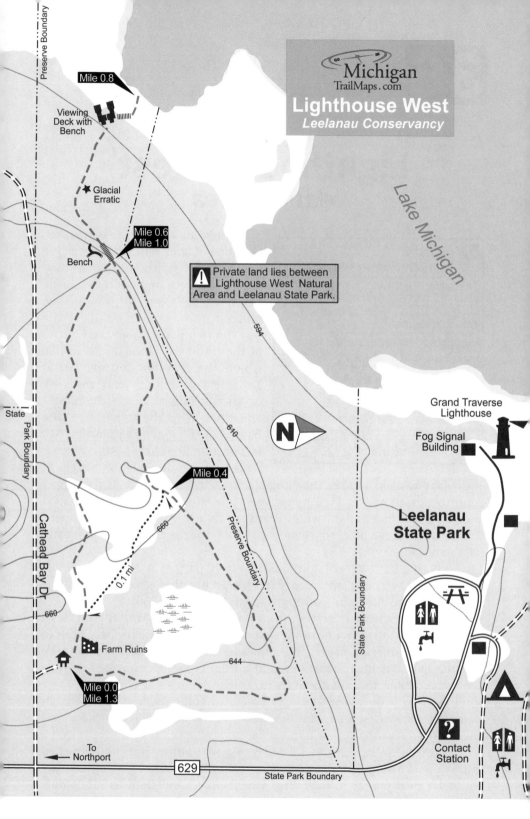

Preserve Boundary

Michigan TrailMaps.com

Lighthouse West
Leelanau Conservancy

Mile 0.8

Viewing Deck with Bench

★ Glacial Erratic

Mile 0.6
Mile 1.0

Bench

⚠ Private land lies between Lighthouse West Natural Area and Leelanau State Park.

594

Lake Michigan

State Park Boundary

610

N

Grand Traverse Lighthouse

Fog Signal Building

Cathead Bay Dr.

Mile 0.4

660

0.1 mi

660

Preserve Boundary

Leelanau State Park

State Park Boundary

Farm Ruins

644

Mile 0.0
Mile 1.3

? Contact Station

To Northport

629

State Park Boundary

makes for a 1.3-mile hike. Note that private property separates Lighthouse West from the state park's campground, lighthouse and day-use area to the north.

Access and Information

From M-22 in Northport, head north on M-201, following the signs for Leelanau State Park. M-201 becomes County Road 640 (also labeled Woolsey Lake Road) and in 1.5 miles continues on County Road 629. Within 5 miles, just before CR-629 ends at the state park entrance, turn left (west) on Cathead Bay Drive, a dirt road. The trailhead (and parking area) for Lighthouse West is posted less than 200 yards on Cathead Bay Drive.

For more information, contact the Leelanau Conservancy (231-256-9665; *leelanauconservancy.org*) or stop at the conservancy office, 105 North First St., in Leland.

On The Trail

Following the trail in a counterclockwise direction from the trailhead, you head north in a lightly forested area before swinging west. Just before the junction with a crossover spur at **Mile 0.4**, the trail enters a field dotted with pear and apple trees from an old orchard. Patches of wild berries, including raspberries and blackberries, are abundant here.

You re-enter the woods and soon skirt the edge of a steep bluff with views of the hardwood forest below and glimpses of Lake Michigan. At **Mile 0.6**, the trail descends the bluff via a stairway with a bench in the middle and bottoms out in a boulder terrace shaded by maple and beech trees. The boulders were deposited after glaciers receded 10,000 years ago, with the trail swinging around the largest "glacial erratic," a rock the size of a small car.

The trail reaches a viewing deck with a bench, where another stairway descends to the shoreline, a cobble beach whose wetland vegetation and shallow waters attracts wading birds and waterfowl. Reached less than a mile from the trailhead, Lake Michigan is quiet, uncrowded and remote, a complete contrast to the often-busy state park just to the north.

To return, backtrack through the boulder terrace, re-climb the stairs and go right at the junction at the top. The last leg of the trail winds through mostly open fields where sparrows, indigo buntings and waxwings can be sighted. Just before the trailhead is reached at **Mile 1.3** is an old plow and other remnants of the farm that once occupied this area.

Crossing a meadow at DeYoung Natural Area in the fall.

37

DeYoung
Natural Area

DeYoung
Distance: 2 miles
Hiking Time: 2 hours
Difficulty: Easy to moderate
Highlights: Historic farm, Cedar Lake, Fishing pier
Map Source: DeYoung Natural Area from MichiganTrailMaps.com or Leelanau Conservancy at leelanauconservancy.org
Trailhead: **GPS** N44° 48' 34.03" W85° 39' 11.89"

For many the quintessential landmark along the way to the Leelanau Peninsula from Traverse City are the barns, outbuildings and Victorian house of the Louis DeYoung farmstead.

The farm straddles Cherry Bend Road, less than 2 miles from M-22, and what was once the Manistee and Northeastern Railroad that is now the popular Leelanau Trail. To generations of locals, the buildings, especially the large barns, indicated they were either escaping the urban clutches of Traverse City or would soon be home again.

The farmstead dates back to the 1860s when Henry Campbell cleared the land and then diverted a stream to power a water wheel. DeYoung purchased the farm in 1925 as a 26-year-old newlywed and remained on it for almost 80 years. A true innovator, DeYoung turned the water wheel powerhouse into a machine shop that included light bulbs before standard electricity service was available in the area. He embraced tractor-powered farming early on and was one of the first in the Leelanau Peninsula to plant cherry trees.

In 2003 at the age of 103, DeYoung turned over decisions to his son in regards to preserving the farm and the mile of undeveloped shoreline on Cedar Lake. Louis DeYoung died a year later, and in 2008 a 145-acre tract that included the farmstead and its historical buildings was acquired by the Leelanau Conservancy.

The farm was an unusual acquisition for a conservancy since the home, barns and powerhouse, dating from 1870 to 1940, still contained furniture, equipment and documents relating to the Campbell and DeYoung families. The Leelanau Conservancy turned to Eastern Michigan University's nationally-recognized Graduate Program in Historic Preservation to assist in documenting the structures and developing a preservation plan. The conservancy also invited local farmers to resume farming and raise livestock in the natural area, using small-scale, sustainable methods such as permaculture and organic farming.

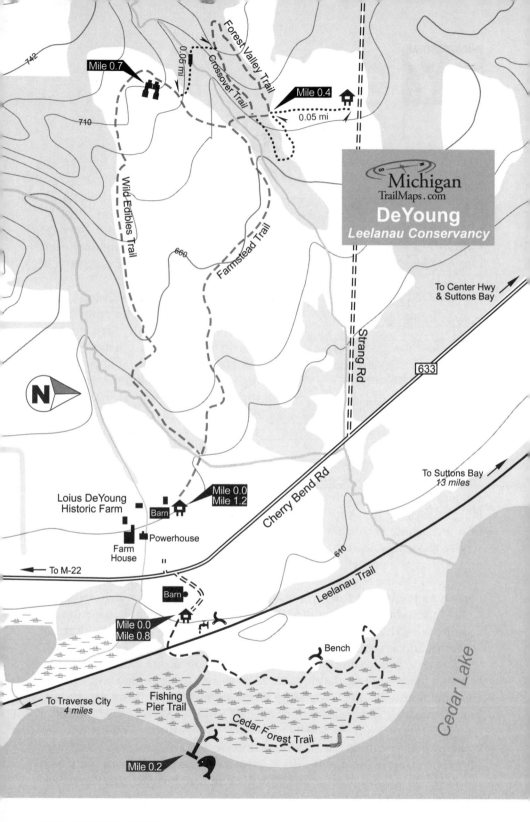

Mile 0.7

0.05 mi

Forest Valley Trail

Crossover Trail

Mile 0.4

0.05 mi

Michigan
TrailMaps.com

DeYoung
Leelanau Conservancy

742

710

660

Wild Edibles Trail

Farmstead Trail

To Center Hwy
& Suttons Bay

Strang Rd

633

N

To Suttons Bay
13 miles

Loius DeYoung
Historic Farm

Mile 0.0
Mile 1.2

Cherry Bend Rd

Barn

Powerhouse

Farm
House

610

Leelanau Trail

To M-22

Barn

Mile 0.0
Mile 0.8

Bench

Cedar Lake

To Traverse City
4 miles

Fishing
Pier Trail

Cedar Forest Trail

Mile 0.2

DeYoung is a work in progress but hikers already have more than 2 miles of trail to explore. On the east side of Cherry Bend Road is the Cedar Forest Trail that makes for a loop of less than a mile and includes a fishing pier and viewing deck on Cedar Lake. On the west side, described here as a 1.2-mile loop, trails first pass the buildings and then skirt small farm fields, upland meadows and stands of hardwoods.

The loops can be combined for an easy 2-mile outing in this unique natural area where farming and outdoor recreation exist side-by-side and naturally complement each other.

Access and Information

From Traverse City, head north on M-22 and then west on Cherry Bend Road (County Road 633). Within 2 miles the DeYoung Natural Area is posted with trailheads on both sides of the road. A third trailhead and parking area is located a third of a mile west on Strang Road. For more information, contact the Leelanau Conservancy (231-256-9665; *leelanauconservancy.org*).

On The Trail

Cedar Forest Trail

On the east side of Cherry Bend Road, in the shadow of a huge barn, is the trailhead and parking for this 0.8-mile loop. There is also a hand pump for drinking water.

The trail immediately crosses the paved Leelanau Trail – *watch for cyclists!* – and begins as the Fishing Pier Trail, the route to Cedar Lake that was transformed into a handicapped accessible path in 2015. The trail quickly passes the junction with the return of Cedar Forest Trail and then uses a long, curved boardwalk to snake through a stand of mature cedars. In less than a quarter mile you pass a bench along the boardwalk and arrive at a huge deck extended out on Cedar Lake.

Built as a fishing pier, the reason for the rod holders, the deck is situated at the edge of a drop-off in the 50-acre lake, making it an idea place to cast a line for smallmouth bass, panfish or perch. It also has benches and serves as a wildlife observation area where on a quiet evening it's possible to see a variety of waterfowl, marsh birds and herons.

Near the boardwalk bench, Cedar Forest Trail departs to the north and winds through a cedar swamp. You're close enough to Cedar Lake to see the shoreline through the trees or even hear an occasional water skier in the summer. At **Mile 0.5** the trail swings south, passes a bench along the edge of the meadow and returns to the handicapped accessible trail.

Farmstead and Wild Edibles Trails

The trails on the west side of Cherry Bend Road were opened in 2013 and are continually being improved. This loop is the most natural route and easiest to follow, much of it marked by blue-tipped posts. The trailhead is just past the restored powerhouse — the Farmstead Trail begins by skirting a

The Cedar Lake fishing pier at DeYoung Natural Area.

small pasture with movable fences that allow livestock to rotationally graze to enrich the soil with nutrients.

After crossing a small stream, head right at the junction as the trail passes through remnants of old farm fields and orchards. Within a third of a mile, the Farmstead Trail swings south and skirts a forest of huge maples that shade the stream in a small ravine before reaching a junction.

Head north (right) to dip into the ravine and cross the stream along the Forest Valley Trail. On the other side of the stream the trail climbs to a junction on the edge of an open meadow from which the trailhead on Strang Road can be seen. Head south (left) to loop back into a wooded ravine along the Crossover Trail, crossing the stream and returning to the junction at **Mile 0.6**.

Wild Edibles Trail continues south to skirt the old orchard and climbs reaches to the high point of the route. Reached at **Mile 0.7**, the grassy ridge rises to 710 feet in elevation to provide a nice view of Louis DeYoung's farm and a slice of Cedar Lake. The trail, so named for what hikers might find to nibble on along the way, including wild blackberries and grapes in late summer, descends off the ridge. You skirt the south side of the old orchard before swinging into the woods and arriving at an old two-track at **Mile 1**. Head east (left) to return to the trailhead in less than a quarter mile.

Other Trails

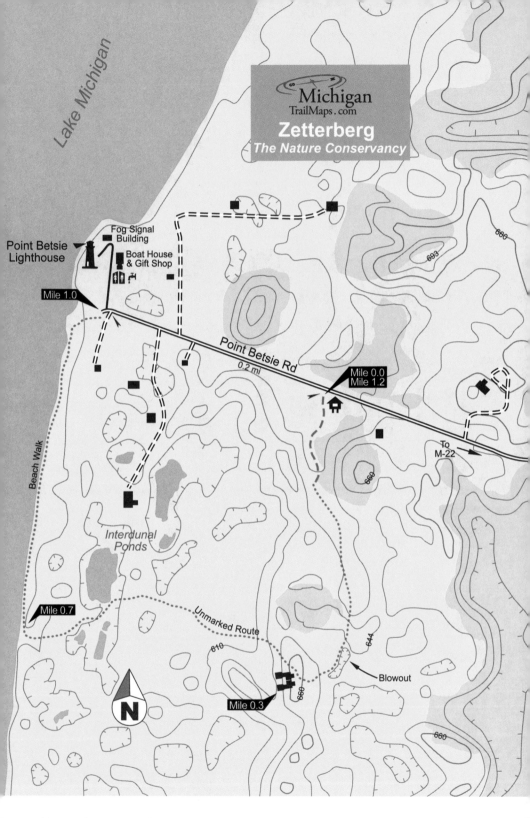

Lake Michigan

Michigan
TrailMaps.com

Zetterberg
The Nature Conservancy

Fog Signal
Building

Point Betsie
Lighthouse

Boat House
& Gift Shop

Mile 1.0

Point Betsie Rd
0.2 mi

Mile 0.0
Mile 1.2

To
M-22

Beach Walk

660

693

660

644

610

660

660

Interdunal
Ponds

Mile 0.7

Unmarked Route

Blowout

Mile 0.3

N

Zetterberg Preserve
The Nature Conservancy

Zetterberg		
Distance: 1.2 miles		
Hiking Time: 1 hour		
Difficulty: Moderate		
Highlights: Historic lighthouse, Beach walk		
Map Source: Zetterberg Preserve from MichiganTrailMaps.com		
Trailhead: **GPS** N44°41' 22.09" W86° 15' 2.0"		

One of the most beloved landmarks in Benzie County, one of the most photographed lighthouses in the country, is Point Betsie Lighthouse

Built in 1858, the lighthouse is located on a wide sweeping point just off M-22, 5 miles north of Frankfort. The red and white tower and lightkeeper's house is framed in by a pair of green pine trees behind it and often a deep blue sky above it, with the Lake Michigan surf rolling in on one side and golden sand everywhere else. In the evening, locals and tourists alike arrive at the beach to watch the sun dip into the shimmering horizon of Lake Michigan in what has become Benzie County's most enduring summer tradition.

But Point Betsie is more than a picturesque lighthouse or a place to watch sunsets. It is also a natural wonder, a dynamic mosaic of shifting sand dunes and Lake Michigan shoreline. The Michigan Chapter of the Nature Conservancy began preserving the sand dune habitat in 1988 when Steve and Connie Zetterberg donated the 71 acres adjacent to the lighthouse. First known as the Point Betsie Natural Preserve, the area has since been enlarged to 100 acres and renamed the Zetterberg Preserve of Point Betsie.

Most of the point is fragile open dune habitat extending a half mile east from Lake Michigan. But the preserve also contains interdunal wetlands and tracts of boreal forest. Flora ranges from Michigan lily, marram grass, beach pea and hoary puccoon in the open dunes to forested islands of balsam fir, paper birch, red oak and creeping juniper. Thriving within the preserve are threatened species such as Pitcher's thistle, fascicled broomrape and the Lake Huron locust.

Point Betsie is also an important resting site for migratory birds and offers excellent birding opportunities during the peak migration periods in May and late August through September. Migrating species include the peregrine falcon while cedar waxwings are often spotted in the pockets of forest and sandpiper and killdeer along the beach.

The Point Betsie Lighthouse, built in 1858 and now a maritime museum.

Other than a short segment of trail that extends south of Point Betsie Road, there are no official foot trails in the Zetterberg Preserve so the Nature Conservancy asks visitors to respect the fragile ecosystem when hiking. The majority of this popular 1.2-mile loop is along the trail, the shoreline and Point Betsie Road, with only a half mile of unmarked route through the open dunes.

Access and Information

From Frankfort, head north on M-22 for 4.5 miles and then west on Point Betsie Road. From M-22, follow Point Betsie Road for a half mile and look for The Nature Conservancy sign on the south side of the road. A trail starts near the sign. You can park on the roadside by the sign, or drive to the end of the road where there is more parking near the lighthouse.

For more information, contact the Friends of Point Betsie Lighthouse (231-352-4915; *www.pointbetsie.org*) or the Michigan Chapter of the Nature Conservancy at (517-316-0300; *www.nature.org*).

On The Trail

From The Nature Conservancy sign, a sandy, soft but still distinct trail heads south, with a stand of pines to the east and open dune country to the west. You skirt the base of a dune briefly, pass a second pocket of pines to the west and then traverse the edge of a small blowout , where the trail fizzles out. Swing to the west and trudge to the top of the dune through the loose sand.

At the crest, reached at **Mile 0.3**, is a view of Lake Michigan straight ahead, the Point Betsie Lighthouse to the northwest and open dune country all around. Descend the dune and head for Lake Michigan along the easiest route between the many small dunes and hills. Mostly likely, you'll pass through a series of interdunal ponds, small seasonal bodies of water that may or may not be there depending on recent rainfall. At **Mile 0.7**, you climb a low ridge and descend to Lake Michigan.

Follow the shoreline north (right) with the impressive tower of the lighthouse guiding you. At **Mile 1**, just before the lighthouse, a sandy path departs the beach and arrives at the parking area. Also located here is the paved trail to the lighthouse and the Boat House Museum. It's a quarter mile east along Point Betsie Road to the trailhead

The Point Betsie Lighthouse

The Point Betsie Lighthouse, marking the southern entrance of the Manitou Passage, was built in 1858 at a cost of $50,000, with the rest of the lifesaving station added 17 years later. The tower was equipped with a fourth-order Fresnel lens that sat 52 feet above the lake and had a range of 27.5 miles. After much lobbying, a fog signal building was added in 1891, with the horn first sounding on New Year's Eve.

Despite Frankfort's location just to the south, Point Betsie was an isolated station without road access. As a foreman of a surveying team noted in 1875: "shifting sands in summer and drifting snows in winter," made any proposed road from the lighthouse to the nearby highway (now M-22) "of little service" so that getting supplies from Frankfort remained easier along the beach or by boat.

The station proved to be an important one. One of the more dramatic rescues recorded was in 1898 when the steamer St. Lawrence was stranded about two miles south of Point Betsie. In a blinding blizzard, the U.S. Life-Saving staff rescued the entire crew with the exception of a man who tried, unsuccessfully, to make it to shore on his own.

Point Betsie, the last manned light on Lake Michigan's eastern shore, was automated by 1984. In 1996, when the light's turning mechanism failed, the fourth-order lens was removed and replaced by a small acrylic lens. Soon after that, Friends of Point Betsie Lighthouse began renovating the structure and by 2006 the exterior was completed. Since then the group has renovated the nearby Fog Signal Building and the Boat House, which houses a gift shop and exhibit room.

The first floor of the lighthouse is a maritime museum focused on the history of the U.S. Life-Saving Service and U.S. Coast Guard at Point Betsie. The most prized exhibit is the fourth-order Fresnel lens that provided the station's sweeping beam for almost a century and was eventually returned by the Coast Guard.

The lighthouse is open from mid-May to mid-October and the small fee to view it includes a guided tour and a trip to the top of the tower. For hours check the Friends of Point Betsie Lighthouse web site (*www.pointbetsie.org*).

Lake Michigan

N

660

Mile 3.7

9

0.25 mi

Pothole
Ridge
Spur

10

11

660

693

Mud Lake Trail

710 ft ▲

Tamarack Cutoff

0.5 mi

8

Mile 2.4

12

Mile 4.5

660

Mile 1.6

610

Mile 1.0

5

Manitou
Overlook

7

684 ft ▲

Maple Ridge Cutoff

0.2 mi

660

13

Mud
Lake

3

4

Handicapped Accessible Trail

2

6

Mile 1.9

Mile 0.75

660

0.3 mi

Lake Michigan Trail

1

Mile 0.0
Mile 5.0

Bench

676 ft ▲

660

Densmore Rd

Michigan
TrailMaps.com

Mud Lake Loop
Leelanau State Park

To
County
Road
629

Woolsey
Memorial
Airport

39

Mud Lake Loop
Leelanau State Park

Leelanau State Park

Distance: 5 miles	
Hiking Time: 2 to 3 hours	
Difficulty: Moderate	
Highlights: Scenic overlook, Lake Michigan shoreline	
Map Source: Leelanau State Park: Lake Michigan/Mud Lake Loop from MichiganTrailMaps.com	
Trailhead: **GPS**	N45° 10' 22.64" W85° 34' 25.17"

After M-22 heads up the west side of the Leelanau Peninsula and reaches the quaint village of Northport it makes a 180-degree turn and goes south toward bustling Traverse City. Hikers and backcountry skiers would do well to continue another 4 miles north from the state highway to the undeveloped slice of one of the most unusual state parks in Michigan.

Preserving the tip of Michigan's "little finger" is Leelanau State Park, best known as the home of the historic Grand Traverse Lighthouse, a place to look for Petoskey stones and for a campground where you can pitch a tent near the edge of Lake Michigan. But the bulk of the 1,350-acre park, including its 6-mile network of trails, is a separate unit that adjoins scenic Cathead Bay and is devoid of the usual state park amenities.

During the summer season peak, when the campground is full and there is a line of visitors waiting to climb the lighthouse tower, the beach and trails at Cathead Bay are uncrowded. No camping or mountain bikes are allowed in this nonmotorized area consisting of low dunes forested predominantly in hardwoods of maple, beech, white ash, and paper birch. Toward the water, the forest gives way to open dunes covered only by patches of beach grass, shrubs, and a few cottonwoods. The shoreline itself is a beautiful beach with fine sand and often a gentle surf.

The trails are easy to follow as they are well marked with locator maps and numbered junctions. Although there are five named trails within the network, the system basically forms a 5-mile loop using the Lake Michigan Trail and Mud Lake Trail, with three crossover spurs in the middle. The Lake Michigan Trail taken to the beach is a 1.7-mile loop while the 4.7-mile trek described here makes for a pleasant 3-hour walk or even a full-day outing if combined with an extended break on the beach.

Birders congregate here in the spring to search Mud Lake for a variety of waterfowl while the hardwoods, whose colors generally peak in early October, make this trail an excellent choice in the fall. The most popular use

The foredunes at Cathead Bay in Leelanau State Park.

of this tract is for Nordic skiing, but in summer it's hard to imagine a better destination for a hike than the relatively isolated beaches of Cathead Bay.

Access and Information

The park is located at the tip of the Leelanau Peninsula, a 30-mile drive from Traverse City along M-22. In Northport, continue north along M-201 and then County Road 629 for another 4 miles. A sign for the trailhead is posted on County Road 629, just past Woolsey Airport, and is reached by turning left on Densmore Road and following it to a parking area at the end. The rest of the park is another 4 miles north on County Road 629.

A daily vehicle permit or annual state park pass is required to park a vehicle at the Cathead Bay Trailhead. For more information, contact Leelanau State Park (231-386-5422).

On The Trail

In the parking area is a large display map of the trail system along with a vault toilet, drinking water and picnic tables. Three trails depart from near the trailhead sign. Mud Lake Trail heads out in a northeasterly direction as a graveled handicapped accessible path, while to the northwest a direct route to Manitou Overlook departs into the woods. Lake Michigan Trail, which is marked by blue boot print symbols, enters the dunes due west.

Lake Michigan Trail provides the easiest avenue to the beach and begins as a level walk through a pine/hardwood stand that keeps you well shaded from the sun. In less than a half mile, you pass the first of several benches and hike through a series of forested dunes. The ridges actually rise above both sides of the trail, but the trek remains surprisingly level. At *Mile 0.7* is the junction with Cathead Spur, the beach access trail.

From there, it's third of a mile out to the bay, along a path that begins in the forest but suddenly breaks out into open dunes. In summer, you'll make the transition from cool forest to brilliant sunlight and hot sand in three steps or less. Yellow posts lead you across the low, rolling dunes to Cathead Bay, a spectacular spot to unroll a beach blanket. Only a few cottages are visible to the east; to the west is Cathead Point, and out on the horizon of Lake Michigan lie the Fox Islands.

Backtrack the spur trail and then head left to continue on Lake Michigan Trail. The trail climbs over a low dune and at **Mile 1.4** reaches the next junction, Manitou Overlook Spur. This side trail to the left is an uphill walk, including a long staircase at the end, to a wooden observation platform and bench where you can view the edge of the forest, open dunes, and the shoreline. Although it's called Manitou Overlook, the most prominent landmark in Lake Michigan is the Fox Islands, and in the still of a quiet morning, they often appear to be floating on a layer of mist and fog.

Backtrack to post No. 4 and continue straight to reach post No. 6 at **Mile 1.9**, which marks the junction with Mud Lake Trail. Marked by orange boot prints, Mud Lake Trail heads left and within a quarter mile reaches post No. 7 and the Maple Ridge Cutoff, a crossover spur that allows you to reach the parking area in a half mile south. There, near the posted map, is a bench overlooking several impressive paper birch trees. The Mud Lake Trail continues in a northerly direction as a wide and level path, reaching post No. 8 and the junction to Tamarack Cutoff at **Mile 2.4**.

Most of the trails are wide tracks to accommodate both hikers and skiers, but the northern half of Mud Lake changes to a true footpath as it winds among several forested dunes. The terrain is interesting and at **Mile 3.3** you begin a steady climb, topping off at a well-placed bench where you can rest and gaze down into a pothole, a natural amphitheater forested in hardwoods. You descend to a marsh, skirt it, and then follow a boardwalk across the middle of the marsh to arrive at post No. 9 at **Mile 3.7**.

This post marks the junction to Pothole Ridge Spur. Mud Lake Trail heads south (left) and is a shorter and more level route. Pothole Ridge begins with the steepest climb of the day — despite what common sense tells you, start climbing. This segment is a scenic walk along the crest of a dune that includes a pair of boardwalks built to prevent excessive erosion to the delicate sides, the second with a pair of built-in benches. You pass post No. 10 and then descend to post No. 11 and the marshy north end of Mud Lake, reached at **Mile 4.2**.

Returning to Mud Lake Trail, head southeast along what was an old two-track that parallels a towering dune on one side while providing glimpses of the marshy shoreline of the lake on the other.

Keep an eye on Mud Lake — a variety of birds and wildflowers, including wild irises, can often be spotted. At **Mile 4.5**, you arrive at post No. 12, marking the junction with Tamarack Cutoff and one end of the handicapped accessible segment. There are also picnic tables among the trees. From here, it's a half mile until Mud Lake Trail emerges into the open field and then enters the east end of the parking lot.

Along the Leelanau Trail the Bay Area Transportation Authority (BATA) offers a Bike-N-Ride program with special buses that transports cyclists and their bikes back to Traverse City or Suttons Bay.

Leelanau Trail
TART Trails

Leelanau Trail	
Distance: 14 miles	
Biking Time: 2 to 4 hours	
Difficulty: Moderate	
Highlights: Paved rail-trail with bus service, vineyards	
Map Source: Leelanau Trail from MichiganTrailMaps.com or TART Trails at traversetrails.org	
Trailhead: **GPS**	N44° 47' 37.15" W85° 38' 44.33"

It's easy to tell when you leave the urban fringe of Traverse City on the Leelanau Trail and enter the rural countryside of the Leelanau Peninsula. The yellow caution signs with "Private Drive" are replaced by a silhouette of a farmer on his tractor. Homes give way to red barns, the buzz of a city fades into the pastoral tranquility of farm fields and cherry orchards.

Who would have thought that the 17-mile rail-trail with such a contentious past would lead to such a peaceful setting?

The rail-trail dates back to 1903 when the Traverse City, Leelanau & Manistique Railroad completed the line to Northport as part of a new car ferry service across Lake Michigan to the Upper Peninsula. The Leelanau Scenic Railway was the last to use the rails. After the service ceased operations in the early 1990s, the Leelanau Trail Association (LTA) was formed in 1994 to purchase 15 miles of rail corridor from Traverse City to Suttons Bay. Almost immediately there was heated opposition by property owners leading to numerous court cases over the proposed trail.

But LTA volunteers forged ahead and by 1997 had paved more than four miles of the trail at its north and south ends and established a large trailhead on Cherry Bend Road. The following year, TART Trails, Inc. was formed and took over the administration of several regional trails, including the Leelanau.

In 2004, the Leelanau Trail was connected to the TART Trail that extends 11 miles to the east through the Traverse City. By 2014, when the Leelanau Trail had become a fully paved, off-road connection between Traverse City and Suttons Bay, winding past picturesque farms and vineyards, forests, lakes and ponds, there was no denying its overwhelming popularity.

Today, local bike shops rent bicycles to out-of-town visitors. The Bay Area Transportation Authority (BATA) offers a Bike-N-Ride program with special buses that take weary cyclists and their bikes back to Traverse City from

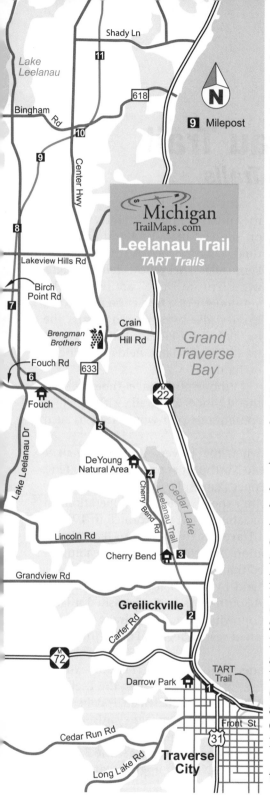

Suttons Bay. Grand Traverse Bike Tours (*www.grandtraversebiketours.com*) incorporates the trail in a self-guided tour of the Leelanau wine country and in the winter TART volunteers groom it from the Cherry Bend trailhead north to Birch Point and from 4th Street in Suttons Bay south to Revold Road for both classic and skate skiing.

The Leelanau Trail officially extends from Carter Road in the Greilickville area of Traverse City to Dumas Road on the north side of Suttons Bay. For many, the trail is a 14-mile ride from the Cherry Bend Trailhead to the trailhead at First and Cedar Streets in Suttons Bay, where riders can park their bikes and walk to almost a dozen restaurants and cafes. After refueling and reviving, it's a ride of less than a half mile to the BATA stop for the bus back to Traverse City.

Access and Information ———

Mileposts along the Leelanau Trail begin with Mile 0 on the TART Trail in Clinch Park, Traverse City's waterfront park overlooking West Grand Traverse Bay. Major trailheads for the Leelanau Trail where you can park a vehicle are located at Cherry Bend Road (Milepost 3), Fouch Road (just before Milepost 6), and 4th Street just west of M-22 in Suttons Bay (Milepost 17). You can also park and pick up the trail at the DeYoung Natural Area on Cherry Bend Road (near Milepost 4) 2 miles from M-22 and near the Keswick Methodist Church, on Center Highway between Fort and Revold Roads (Milepost 14).

During the summer months, there are portable toilets at the

DeYoung Natural Area and public restrooms at the Suttons Bay Marina. The restrooms at Inland Seas Education Association, located across M-22 next to Boone's Restaurant, are available to trail users year-round when the office is open Monday through Friday from 9 a.m. to 5 p.m.

The Bay Area Transportation Authority (BATA) Bike-N-Ride program allows you to pedal the Leelanau Trail one-way and ride the bus back in either direction to your starting point. Weekday service is offered from late June

Bay Area Transportation Authority

to Labor Day, with the every-other-hour Bike-n-Ride beginning at the Hall Street Transfer Station at 5:30 a.m. and ending at 6:30 p.m. More limited weekend service is available from late May to late October. In Suttons Bay, the BATA stop is at the Suttons Bay Library on Front Street.

Bikes are transported as part of a regular $3 fare that is paid on the bus in cash or with a BATA FlashFare card. It's first-come-first-serve so on the weekends during the height of the tourist season it's wise to get to the stops early. For a complete list of stops and times, contact BATA (231-941-2324; *bata.net/bikenride*).

For more information or cycling events staged on the Leelanau Trail, contact TART Trails (231-941-4300; *www.traversetrails.org*).

On The Trail

The Cherry Bend Road trailhead at **Milepost 3** has parking for a dozen cars, with the lot often full on summer weekends. There is an information kiosk at the trailhead but no toilets or drinking water. The BATA bus stop is across the street at Leelanau Studios, 10781 E Cherry Bend Rd., or a third of a mile west of M-22.

At this point, the Leelanau Trail heads north along the west side of Cedar Lake. The best chance to view the lake is at the DeYoung Natural Area just beyond **Milepost 4**. The trailhead includes a hand pump for drinking water, an edible trail garden and a trail of less than a quarter mile to a fishing pier on the lake (see page 175). In another 1.5 miles is the Fouch Road Trailhead on County Road 614.

The Leelanau Trail immediately crosses CR-641, passes **Milepost 6** and enters the rural heart of Leelanau County. Bikers ride past cherry orchards, apple trees and corn fields, often separated by small woodlots, enjoying the best feature of rail-trails, a lack of steep topography.

There are two noticeable changes in elevation along the trail, but both are gentle downhills while heading north. The first is near Bingham, the halfway point of the ride, where the trail utilizes a classic railroad trestle to cross Center Highway just before **Milepost 10**. Beyond it is a raised rail bed, with rolling orchards and pastures on each side of you, as the trail descends for a half mile into a forest of young maples and beeches.

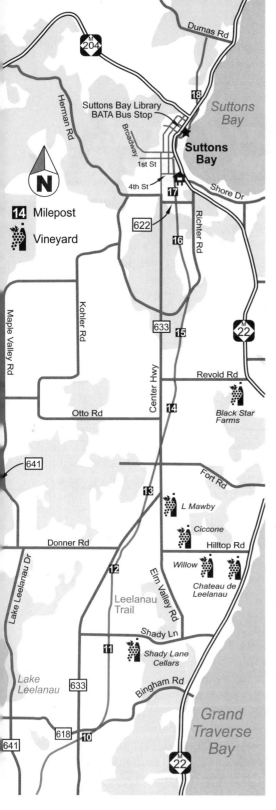

Just beyond **Milepost 11**, you cross Shady Lane, where you can detour to the east for a third of a mile to visit the tasting room of Shady Lane Cellars (*www.shadylanecellars.com*), one of a half-dozen vineyards within easy riding distance of the trail. The Leelanau Trail crosses Center Highway a second time before **Milepost 13** where there again is an opportunity to depart briefly and visit up to four vineyards. The closest is L. Mawby (*lmawby.com*), less than a half mile away on Elm Valley Road.

A half mile beyond **Milepost 14** you cross Revold Road and begin the second descent of the day, a stretch where the pedaling is easy and the views are the most extensive of the ride. For more than 2 miles you gently coast downhill until bottoming out at CR-622. On the other side of the street is a level stretch of trail that leads into the heart of Suttons Bay. The 4th Street Trailhead and **Milepost 17** is reached within a third of a mile. A block beyond that, on the corner of 1st Street and Cedar Street, is the Leelanau Trail Kiosk, with information and bicycle racks.

From the kiosk, Suttons Bay's shops, cafes, ice cream parlors and beach on Grand Traverse Bay are a short walk away. To reach the rest of the Leelanau Trail, head west on 1st Street for a block and then north (right) on Marys Street. Within three blocks, turn east (right) on Jefferson Street and follow it to the corner of Front Street and Adams Street where the Leelanau Trail resumes by winding around the Suttons Bay Library.